S0-AFQ-667

From Afar to Zulu

ALSO AVAILABLE FROM WALKER AND COMPANY

From Abenaki to Zuni: A Dictionary of Native American Tribes by
Evelyn Wolfson

From
AFAR
to
ZULU

A DICTIONARY
OF
AFRICAN CULTURES

Jim Haskins
and
Joann Biondi

WALKER AND COMPANY

NEW YORK

6899199

Copyright © 1995 by Jim Haskins and Joann Biondi

All rights reserved. No part of this book may be reproduced or transmitted in any form or by any means, electronic or mechanical, including photocopying, recording, or by any information storage and retrieval system, without permission in writing from the Publisher.

First published in the United States of America in 1995 by Walker Publishing Company, Inc.

Published simultaneously in Canada by Thomas Allen & Son Canada. Limited, Markham, Ontario

Library of Congress Cataloging-in-Publication Data
Haskins, James, 1941–
From Afar to Zulu : a dictionary of African cultures / Jim Haskins and Joann Biondi.
p.   cm.
ISBN 0-8027-8290-6 (hardcover). — ISBN 0-8027-8291-4 (reinforced)
1. Ethnology—Africa—Dictionaries.   2. Africa—Social life and customs—Dictionaries.   I. Biondi, Joann.   II. Title.
GN645.H27   1995
306′.096—dc20   94-11545
CIP

The illustrations throughout this book are linocuts based on traditional African motifs and patterns. All illustrations are by Geoffrey Williams and appear courtesy of Dover Publications.

Photographs on the following pages used by permission of the National Museum of African Art, Eliot Elisofon Photographic Archives, Smithsonian Institution. Unless otherwise indicated, the photographs were taken by Elisofon himself. Page 2 (from the Pères Blancs [White Father's] Mission Collections), 17, 18, 19, 39, 45, 50, 51, 52, 53, 58 and 59 (both by Agbenyega Adedze), 73, 74, 78, 79, 80, 95, 96, 110, 116 (by Thomas Weir), 120, 121, 126 (by Edmond Fortier), 131, 135, 153, 154, 155, 160, 165 (by Bonnevide Studio), 166 (by Edmond Fortier), 167 (by David Wason Ames), 169, 170, 171.
Photographs on pages 7, 85, and 179 appear courtesy of the New York Public Library Picture Collection.
The photograph on page 12 is from the United Nations, used by permission of the Schomburg Center for Research in Black Culture, New York Public Library.
Photographs on pages 13 and 26 used by permission of UPI/Bettmann.
Photographs on pages 46 (from Wide World Photos), 105 (from the *New York Times*), 127, 132, and 178 appear courtesy of the National Archives, Smithsonian Institution.
The photograph on page 63 used by permission of AP/Wide World Photos.
The photographs on pages 104 and 144 appear courtesy of the Library of Congress.

BOOK DESIGN BY GLEN M. EDELSTEIN

Printed in the United States of America

2   4   6   8   10   9   7   5   3

Contents

Acknowledgments

THE AUTHORS WISH TO THANK THE FOLLOWING PEOPLE FOR THEIR assistance: Olabiyi Yai, Department of African Studies, University of Florida; Dan Reboussian, archivist, University of Florida African Area Studies Library; Ann Prewitt, American Museum of Natural History; Henrietta M. Smith, University of South Florida; Deidre Grafel; Diane Hamilton, photo researcher; Kathy Benson; and Ann Kalkhoff.

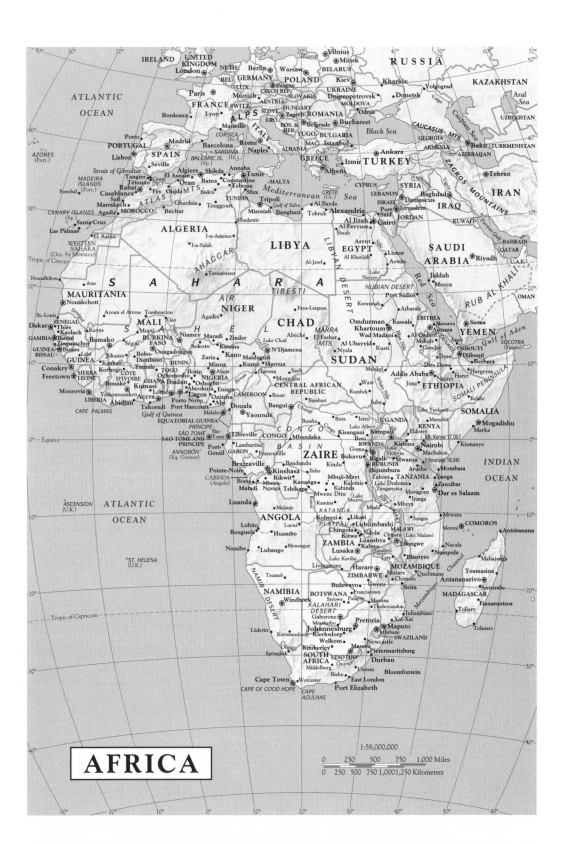

AFRICA

1:58,000,000

0   250   500   750   1,000 Miles

0 250 500 750 1,000 1,250 Kilometers

From Afar to Zulu

Introduction

AFRICA IS A VAST AND VARIED CONTINENT WITH MORE ETHNIC groups than any other place on earth. Anthropologists estimate that there are hundreds of these groups, each with its own history, culture, and customs. Some of the ethnic groups in Africa have thrived for thousands of years and were highly developed societies centuries before the Greek and Roman empires came into being. Others arose in the past few hundred years as a means of adjusting and assimilating to the changing world around them.

Whether they belong to an ethnic group that is several thousand or several hundred years old, most of the people of Africa are the product of the three distinct cultures—indigenous African, Islamic, and European—that have overlapped, coexisted, or merged throughout the continent. Although it is common to describe the indigenous African ethnic groups as tribes, it was the European explorers who chose to use this term. *Tribe* is not a native African expression.

At least 50,000 years ago the species of *Homo sapiens*, to which all the peoples of the world belong today, existed in Africa. By 5000 B.C. Africans had established organized communities of farmers and herders, and as early as 1000 B.C. African societies were engaged in active commerce with each other. By A.D. 1000, several Muslim societies had established themselves in Africa, and many Africans converted to the Islamic religion and way of life. A few hundred years later, European colonizers would bring even more dramatic changes for the peoples of the continent.

By the 1400s, Africans began trading with Europeans who

A Christian family from Burundi, circa 1910.

sought natural resources as well as slaves. In the centuries that followed, Europeans as well as Africans captured, enslaved, and shipped millions of Africans off to work in South America, the Caribbean, and North America. At the same time, many native ethnic groups splintered and formed subgroups, others merged to form larger ones, and many fought against and conquered each other.

During the 1800s and early 1900s, the French, British, Dutch, Spanish, Belgians, and Germans established colonial rule in Africa, further subjugating the African peoples. This European colonial expansion left original native lands divided and reapportioned, and created new nations with little regard to the boundaries of native African ethnic groups. It also imposed a new religion—Christianity—on many of the indigenous peoples, along with a Christian missionary school system.

During the 1960s, a national independence movement swept across the continent, and many new African governments, with African rather than European leaders, were established. New public elementary schools were created, as were technical training centers, mobile school units for nomadic children, and universities.

The African cultures described in this dictionary are the most well-known and historically significant native ethnic groups in Africa today. Although they are only a portion of all the ethnic groups that exist in Africa, as a whole they represent the diverse cultures that are indigenous to the continent. The cultures of the islands off the coasts of Africa, such as Madagascar where the population is chiefly related to Indonesia, are intentionally excluded. Also omitted are in-depth descriptions of the nonnative cultures, such as the Afrikaners in South Africa who are of Dutch descent, and the Arab cultures of Mediterranean Africa, such as the Egyptians, who have closer ties to the Middle East. A few of the cultures described in this book have only 50,000 people, but most have populations of over one million.

This book is intended to be a reference tool for young readers, a clear and simple source of information on Africa's most populous and well-known native cultures. In each entry, the culture's name is spelled phonetically. There are descriptions of the culture's history, environment, villages, homes, social structure, diet, clothing, and religious beliefs. Most headings at the top of each entry are expanded upon in the text. Primary foods are listed in each heading in the approximate order of their importance.

Although the entries are as accurate as research permits, it should be noted that the history and customs of African cultures are not well documented. Much of the material found in books originally comes from the oral traditions of Africans, who have passed their history down from generation to generation through folktales, legends, and fables. Much of it also comes from colonial and post-colonial European scholars, who often wrote about African culture from their own European perspective.

A listing of over 200 additional native cultures and the countries where they live follows the individual entries. To assist those who seek more information, a bibliography of sources used to compile this dictionary is provided. A glossary of foreign and difficult terms is also included.

This dictionary does not pretend to include all aspects of African history or culture. Its purpose is to provide an introduction to native African cultures, and to inspire readers to learn more about the subject.

AFAR
(uh 'far or afar)

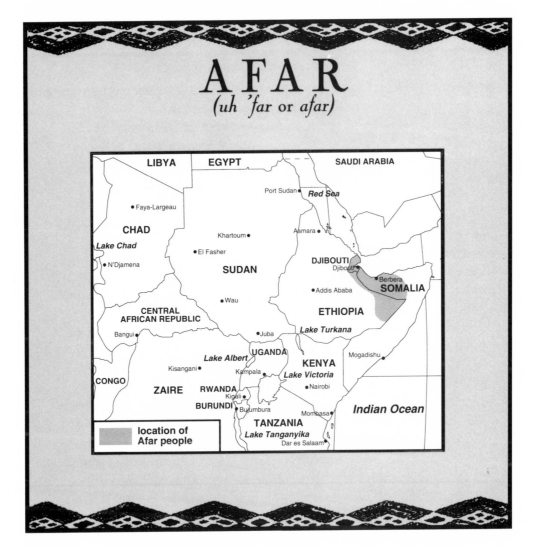

POPULATION:	350,000
LOCATION:	Northern Somalia, Djibouti, southern Ethiopia
LANGUAGE:	Afar, a Cushitic (northeastern African) language
PRIMARY FOODS:	Milk, lamb, goat, beef, *burri* (papyrus root)

THE AFAR LIVE IN THE DRY, ROCKY FLATLAND LOCATED BETWEEN the steep slopes of Ethiopia and the southern end of the Red Sea. This region is also known as the Afar Plain and the Danakil Desert. In fact, when Arab traders first encountered these nomadic peoples sometime between A.D. 1000 and 1500, they referred to them as the Danakil.

Since perhaps 3000 B.C., these independent people have resisted being governed by others and have inhabited the harsh terrain of broken rock and crumbling lava flows where temperatures can reach 135 degrees Fahrenheit and rainfall amounts to less than seven inches per year. Since about A.D. 1500, the Afar have been divided into two groups. The Asemara (Reds), who were the more dominant politically, settled primarily in the area of Assayita, whereas the Ademara (Whites) settled in the remaining, more inhospitable areas of the desert.

Many of the Afar still live as nomads and build easily movable, oval-shaped huts called *aris*. They construct these huts out of sticks, which are cut by the men and then bent and tied together to form the frame of the shelter. Mats are placed on top of the frame. A single mat, used for a door, is kept rolled up and out of the way in the daytime. Inside, a comfortable and cool bed is made of skins spread atop a layer of springy sticks all supported by a framework of forked sticks. The men also build fenced enclosures for their livestock.

A small number of Afar live in apartment buildings in the Ethiopian capital of Addis Ababa, where they remain year-round and work in government jobs such as the Afar broadcasts of the Ethiopian radio station. But many of the Afar live as nomads and spend much of the year on the move because the meager vegetation that appears after the rains is quickly depleted by their livestock. During the rainy season, they move to higher land to avoid both mosquitoes and flooding; but as the dry season returns, they move back to the riverbanks or permanent water holes created by underground streams.

The Afar diet consists mainly of the milk and meat of their livestock but also includes a porridge made of milk and burri (papyrus root), and heavy round pancakes made of wheat topped with red pepper and a sauce of clarified butter called *ghee*. By trading

Afar men pry slabs of salt from an ancient seabed in the Danakil Depression, Ethiopia.

ghee and the salt they collect from deposits in the desert, they may also obtain other grains such as millet, which is so scarce that it is roasted and eaten a few grains at a time. Ghee is used in religious ceremonies and as a cosmetic. Milk is so important to the Afar that it is also used as a social offering, given to visitors to establish a proper guest-host relationship.

An important part of Afar culture is the initiation into manhood, an event that usually takes place when a boy reaches the age of 15. A group of boys will undergo circumcision and immediately afterward be expected to call out the names of any livestock they can remember. The boys are then given the animals whose names they have recited. This rite of passage ends with a feast. In the past, a further requirement for achieving manhood was to kill a male member of an enemy tribe. The young Afar man was then looked upon with respect and entitled to certain rights, such as marriage. The violence of this custom, which faded centuries ago, is a reflection of the great importance placed on bravery and strength, qualities crucial to survival in a harsh environment. Like the boys, Afar girls get circumcised as teenagers, as an initiation into womanhood.

Clothing of Afar men is the traditional *sanafil,* a white cloth wrapped at the waist and tied at the right hip. A curved dagger called a *jile* is also a traditional part of the man's dress. This dagger, which is hung across the chest, is about 15 inches long, with a double-edged blade. Afar women also wear a sanafil tied at the hip, but theirs is dyed brown. Married women may also wear a black strip of cloth called a *shash* on their heads. Young children usually go without clothing.

Labor is divided between men and women, with certain tasks traditionally performed by each. Women tend the sheep, cows, and goats, and look after the camp. Men care for the camels and donkeys and dismantle the camp when it is time to move on. Men also attend to any building tasks.

Because of their location along the coast of Africa near the Arabian peninsula, the Afar were influenced early in their history by the Islamic religion. They do not eat pork and rarely drink alcohol. All of them are Muslim, and some fast for the holy month of Ramadan. Those who can afford to do so make the pilgrimage to the holy Muslim city of Mecca in Saudi Arabia at least once in their lifetime.

Afar also follow the Muslim practice of using only the right hand to eat, accept gifts, and shake hands. The left hand is reserved for sanitary uses such as wiping excrement from the body; using it for other purposes is considered a dreadful insult. This symbolism of right and left can also be found in the dress of the Afar, with the man's sanafil always tied on the right hip.

The Afar retain some aspects of their older, pre-Islam faith, including beliefs in trees and groves that have sacred powers and religious rites such as anointing their bodies with butter or ghee. Like many other African cultures, they believe in the power of the spirits of the dead and celebrate an annual feast of the dead called *Rabena*.

AMHARA
(am 'ha ra)

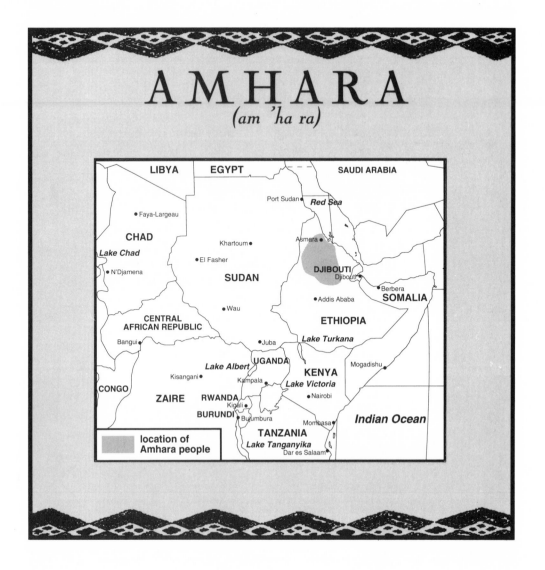

LIBYA · EGYPT · SAUDI ARABIA · Port Sudan · *Red Sea* · Faya-Largeau · CHAD · *Lake Chad* · Khartoum · Asmara · N'Djamena · El Fasher · DJIBOUTI · Djibouti · SUDAN · Berbera · SOMALIA · Wau · Addis Ababa · ETHIOPIA · CENTRAL AFRICAN REPUBLIC · *Lake Turkana* · Bangui · Juba · *Lake Albert* · UGANDA · Mogadishu · Kisangani · Kampala · KENYA · *Lake Victoria* · CONGO · ZAIRE · RWANDA · Nairobi · Kigali · BURUNDI · Bujumbura · *Indian Ocean* · Mombasa · TANZANIA · *Lake Tanganyika* · Dar es Salaam

location of Amhara people

POPULATION:	12,000,000
LOCATION:	Central and northern highlands of Ethiopia
LANGUAGE:	Amharic
PRIMARY FOODS:	Barley, wheat, corn, millet, beans, lentils, vegetables, milk, *injera* bread

THE PEOPLE KNOWN AS THE AMHARA LIVE IN THE CENTRAL AND northern highlands of Ethiopia. Their homeland is a geographically diverse area stretching from Addis Ababa, the capital of Ethiopia, to Lake Tana, Ethiopia's largest lake and the source of the Blue Nile. The topography of the region includes lowlands, steep mountain ranges, fertile plateaus, and tablelands. The highlands in the northwest are separated from the lowlands by the Great Rift Valley. Climate is mild, with a rainy season during the months of December through February that provides the region with 40–50 inches of rain. The forests of the high plateau have been cleared for agricultural use, and this deforestation, along with overgrazing, has resulted in flooding and soil erosion during the rainy season.

The Amhara are descended from the Abyssinians, or early Ethiopians, and Arabic traders of the sixth century B.C. Various other groups from southwest Arabia as well as Semitic peoples (Jews and Arabs of Caucasian ancestry from the eastern Mediterranean area) also settled in Abyssinia, and the intermingling of these groups produced a new civilization, which combined African traditions with those of southern Arabia.

In the first century A.D., the first kingdom established was Aksum, whose people were primarily traders who traveled far inland in search of gold and ivory. They traded at the port of Adulis on the Red Sea. Traders from many other ports visited and settled in Aksum as well. By the fourth century, many Christian missionaries had moved to the area, and their influence led to the spread of Christianity, which separates Ethiopia from its mostly Muslim neighbors.

After years of infighting, the first Amhara emperor, Yenuno Amalak, restored unity in 1270. A long succession of rulers of Aksum followed, all claiming divine rights as the direct descendants of the royal couple Solomon and Sheba. The fall of the emperor Haile Selassie in 1974 marked the end of this long line. In 1987, under the leadership of Lieutenant Colonel Mengistu Haile Mariam, Ethiopia established a new Communist government, and the Amhara lost their status as the ruling class of the country. Although the Amhara no longer control the government, they are still a prominent group and represent 25 percent of the overall population of Ethiopia.

Amhara men work the soil with huge forks in the highlands of Ethiopia.

Originally, the social structure of the Amhara was based on a feudal class society, with the emperor at the top, followed by a landed class, the clergy, merchants and farmers, artisans, tanners, potters, and metalsmiths. At the bottom of this caste system were the freed slaves. Today, the caste system is not as rigid, and there are no longer any freed slaves to occupy the bottom of the caste system.

The Coptic church, a blend of Christian doctrines and ancient beliefs which originated in Egypt and Libya, plays a strong role in the lives of Amharans. Children are baptized in it, and most Amharans observe the obligation of partial fasting two days a week when only one meal a day is eaten, and that meal cannot include any meat, eggs, or dairy products. The influence of the church can be seen in

Haile Selassie in 1957.

traditional Amharan painting, music, and literature. Sadly, poverty and lack of education have led to a decline in Amharan arts and crafts.

The family is still the most important social unit, and extended families tend to live in the same community. Families arrange marriages and expect young couples to have long engagements. Young people in the cities have more choice in whom they marry, but divorce is forbidden by the church in both cities and rural areas.

In the countryside, the Amharan live in kin-based villages. Houses are built around a central marketplace with farms taking up the outlying areas. Each village has its own government— the *kebele,* or town council—which is responsible for settling land disputes and maintaining order in the community.

The traditional house in these areas is the *tukul,* a cone-shaped hut made of clay and straw, with a roof of thatched bamboo. The floor is packed earth. Furniture is sparse, with a few stools, some rugs or furs for sleeping on, and a stone fireplace which the women use for cooking. As Amharans moved to the cities, the tukul gave way to a one-room house built of plaster-covered wood with a corrugated metal roof.

Today, wealthy Amharans living in cities such as Addis Ababa, Gondar, and Harer reside in high-rise apartment buildings with air-conditioning and other modern conveniences. Their children attend either public or private schools where classes are taught in Amharic, the official language of Ethiopia. Once they reach the third or fourth grade, most Amharan schoolchildren start taking English lessons.

Owing to the poor transportation system in the country, children who live in the rural areas rarely have the opportunity to attend school.

Farmers, using a wooden scratch-plow, terracing tools, and simple irrigation systems, grow mainly cereal grains such as hops, wheat, millet, barley, and teff. Teff is ground into flour to make a huge, flat, pancakelike bread called *injera*, the mainstay of the Amharan diet. The barley is slightly fermented to produce a drink called *talla.* Some vegetables, such as cabbage and pumpkin, are also eaten. The Amharan diet contains very little meat. Finely sliced meat may be served on Sundays or at special feasts. Farm animals are used mainly for their dairy products and as beasts of burden, and are rarely slaughtered for meat unless they become too old for farming.

Farming is considered man's work, and all men across the social strata, including priests, do some farming. The Amharan family unit is patriarchal, descending through the father's line, and women occupy a subordinate position. They are not as oppressed as women in some other African cultures, however, and can own land and take their grievances to the kebele.

Cooking is woman's work. They prepare highly aromatic dishes using garlic, mustard seed, fennel, and *barbare,* a famous Ethiopian red cayenne pepper. The injera bread is served with *wot*, a puree of chickpeas, cayenne, and minced onion. Except for ghee, very few animal products are prepared, and the Amharan diet is somewhat deficient in protein.

The *shamma,* a shawl draped over the arm and shoulder, is worn by both men and women. Underneath this togalike cloth, women wear a loose dress called a *kamis.* Men wear either white pants or shorts. In colder weather, a woolen cloak called a *barnos* is added. Just as city-dwelling Amharans may live in Western-style houses, they often wear Western-style clothing, although even in the cities Amharan men are likely to wear a shamma over their suits.

ASHANTI

(ah 'shan tee)

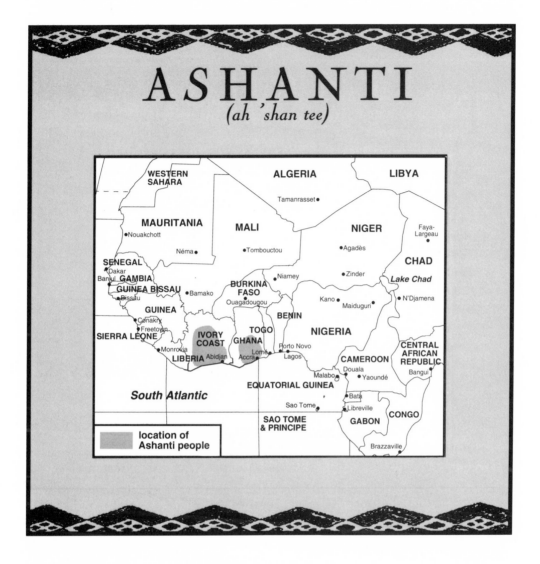

location of
Ashanti people

POPULATION:	1,000,000
LOCATION:	Ghana and the Ivory Coast
LANGUAGE:	Twi
PRIMARY FOODS:	Yams, cassava, shea butter, cereal, vegetables

THE ASHANTI PEOPLE SETTLED IN THE AREA KNOWN TODAY AS south-central Ghana and the Ivory Coast. It is a region of contrasts. The northern part includes a savanna and woodland with large areas of grasses and short, stubby evergreen trees. At times this area is subject to a hot, dry wind called the *harmattan*. Temperatures are usually hot during the day and cool at night. The southern area falls in the equatorial zone and is very warm and humid, having 70–80 inches of rainfall annually. Lake Bosumtwi, the largest in Ghana, is only about 20 miles from the heartland of the Ashanti, the city of Kumasi in the south. This once fertile land and forest have been greatly damaged by slash-and-burn agriculture, a method of clearing land that calls for the cutting down and burning of trees and brush to create a rich bed of soil for seeds to be planted in.

The ancestors of the Ashanti were the Akan people, who developed the Twi language and migrated to the forest areas more than 2,000 years ago. Having settled along a trade route to the goldfields in the southern forest area, they divided into clans according to family lines. Under the leadership of shrewd rulers, they prospered through trade and agriculture. By the time Portuguese traders arrived in the late 1400s, they were already a powerful group of states, the Twifo, the Adansi, and the Kenkyira.

Sometime before 1600, a group of Akan farmers of the Oyoko clan began to move north in search of more farmland. Led by a wise and able leader, Obiri Yeboa, they settled near Lake Bosumtwi in a forested area and became successful producing and trading gold and kola nuts to northern merchants as well as merchants along the coast. They were soon joined by other clans, which were easily assimilated into their thriving community. Eventually, the various families banded together to become the Ashanti, and their growing village became the town of Kumasi.

During the 1600s, however, another group, the powerful Denkyira, periodically challenged the unity of this group, demanding tribute from the Ashanti in the form of taxes on slaves and gold. The Ashanti remained under the sway of the Denkyira until a powerful chief, Osei Tutu of Kumasi, made strong alliances among the various clans. A brilliant administrator, Tutu established a union of clans, created a constitution to preserve that union, and built a

Ashanti woman shaping clay pots, Kumasi, Ghana.

Professional Ashanti carvers from Kumasi, Ghana, make stools to order.

strong army. Under him, the union thrived by mining gold and capturing slaves from weaker cultures. Tutu also firmly established the
Oyoko lineage of Ashanti rulers when he claimed that a golden stool
had fallen from the sky into his lap—a sign of divine election. There-
after, all Ashanti rulers, or *Asantahene* as they were called, were "en-
stooled" on this golden throne, which became a powerful symbol of
the unit and spirit of the Ashanti people.

The next Ashanti ruler, Opoku Ware, continued to advance the
reputation of the Ashanti as a powerful, warlike people, and under
his leadership the Ashanti kingdom enjoyed its strongest period in
history. Kumasi became a great center of political, religious, and in-
tellectual life. As a destination for traders, merchants, and envoys

from other capitals, Kumasi benefited from the influx of skills and knowledge brought by these outsiders. Especially influential were the Muslims, who introduced the Arabic language and the sciences.

The golden stool remains the highest symbol of authority, and it is represented in local villages by a wooden stool, which symbolizes the authority of the village chief. The duties of the chief include caring for ancestral stools and making sacrifices to the stools on important occasions, as well as tending to the political and economic decisions that affect his village.

Today, the Ashanti are an important political force within the state of Ghana, and their territory, in the south-central area of the country, functions as a semi-independent federal region. The current government has been in place since 1981, and although the president, Jerry Rawlings, is not an Ashanti, he has the support of many Ashanti chiefs who approve of his strict economic policies.

In Ghanian cities such as Kumasi, the capital of Ashanti culture, the Ashanti live in apartments or bungalows shared by the extended family. They wear Western-style clothing and have established modern institutions including universities, museums, art galleries, and cultural centers. Although only a tiny percentage of Ashanti ever achieve a secondary or university-level education, many attend primary schools in the cities.

Rural Ashanti build

Ya-Na, paramount chief of the province of North Ghana, on a state visit in 1971. The leather and fur amulets contain writings from the Koran.

Bird design from an Ashanti brass urn, Ghana.

huts of mud and wattle or adobe brick, which are then covered by a thatch or corrugated metal roof. These huts are arranged in rectangular compounds to accommodate the extended families of a clan. Ashanti clans, called *abusu,* are groups of families who follow a matrilineal descent, tracing their lineage to a common female ancestor. Families occupy two residences, with the wife living with her parents and her children and the husband living with his mother's sisters and his uncles. At around eight to ten years of age, when the oldest

Ashanti ceremonial ivory spoon, Ghana.

Ashanti printing stamp patterns.

child in the family is grown up enough to need a father's attention, the wife moves in with her husband's family. The Ashanti believe that children gain their spirit, *ntoro,* from their father, and their clan membership from their mother's blood, *mogya.*

Villagers tend to wear traditional clothing. Men dress in a sleeveless, togalike garment. Women wrap a length of brightly colored fabric around their bodies as well as their hair and adorn themselves with traditional jewelry of fused copper, gold, and silver. Both men and women wear leather sandals on occasion. The village chief always wears sandals, for it is believed that for a chief to walk barefoot brings famine. The chief also wears a crown decorated with gold and beads or a skullcap.

Labor is divided between women and men. Women do the cooking, look after the children, and sell produce in the village. They cook outdoors. The mainstay of the Ashanti diet is a starch base of cereal topped with a vegetable stew called *mash and sauce.* The Ashanti sometimes eat shellfish purchased at markets and drink a great deal of beer.

Ashanti men tend the land and weave the famous, traditional *kente* cloth. Usually worn at festivals and celebrations, it is a brightly

Ashanti patterns from gold weights made of bronze.

colored, intricately patterned cloth woven of cotton or silk. The Ashanti are renowned not only for kente cloth but for a variety of other crafts as well. Their carved wooden sculptures, *ntumpane* (talking drums), and carved terra-cotta figures are also well-known, as is their jewelry made of gold, copper, and silver, and brass weights, which were originally made to weigh the gold dust mined by the Ashanti and which are now collector's items.

In some crafts, there has traditionally been a strict division between women and men. Women can spin thread into cloth, but only men can weave. In pottery making, only men can create dishes, pots, or pipes in human forms.

Many Ashanti crafts reflect the importance of religion and religious ritual in Ashanti life. The worship of the spirits of the dead is the most important expression of religious faith, followed by worship of the golden stool, the spirit not only of Ashanti union but also of the entire Ashanti people.

BAGANDA
('bu ghan dah)

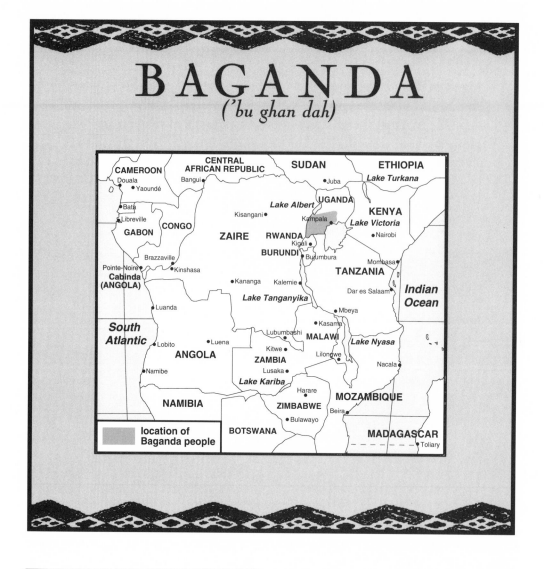

location of Baganda people

POPULATION:	1,000,000
LOCATION:	Uganda
LANGUAGES:	Luganda, English
PRIMARY FOODS:	Plantain, some vegetables, fish, chicken

THE BAGANDA PEOPLE SETTLED ON THE EQUATOR IN WHAT IS now southern Uganda. The region is bowl shaped and surrounded by a ring of mountains on the south side. Also on the southern edge is Lake Victoria. The average altitude is approximately 4,000 feet, and the climate is mild. This mild climate, along with rich soil and an abundance of water, makes the area especially good for agriculture. The Baganda are thus able to produce crops not only for themselves but also for cash and export.

The Baganda trace their founding to Kintu, a legendary leader of the Binto people. The Binto lived in northern and western Uganda during the early 1300s and were very skilled at aggressive military tactics. Kintu and his followers migrated eastward during the 13th century and settled among farmers and herders along the northwest side of Lake Victoria. The kingdom of Baganda eventually grew from this settlement.

Until the 17th century, the kingdom remained small, and power was divided among three *kabakas* (kings). During the 17th century, the three kabakas joined together and thus unified the Baganda around the lake. United in this way, they were also able to increase the territory of Baganda. In the middle of the 18th century, Semakokiro, a very powerful kabaka, established one kingdom under his leadership. Kabakas who succeeded Semakokiro managed to retain complete power and established the Baganda as having the largest kingdom in East Africa.

Another great kabaka, Mutesa, ascended to power in the 19th century. Under his rule, the Baganda saw both military and economic growth. Mutesa divided the kingdom into 10 provinces and established a hierarchy of power. Each province was under the charge of a governor, and within each province were further territorial divisions, or districts, which were overseen by chiefs whose duty was to collect taxes. As a result of this organization, the Baganda gained a reputation as good administrators. After the British moved into Uganda in the late 1800s, they gave the Kingdom of Baganda considerable independence and allowed the kabaka to remain king as long as he obeyed the British governor.

The British in Africa were interested in the crops that could be grown for export and cash, and the Baganda were in a good position to benefit from that interest. The climate of Uganda has always been good for agriculture, and because of their good agricultural skills, most of them today live in self-sufficient villages and small towns. The security afforded them by their rich agricultural base has allowed for the development of a unique lifestyle in which the men are able to move about from village to village and to have more than one family.

Former Ugandan president Idi Amin in air force uniform at a military parade in Kampala, 1975.

This history of self-sufficiency has contributed to the Baganda's independent nature and involvement in national politics. During the Ugandan independence movement in the early 1960s, the Baganda considered seceding from the new nation. To keep peace in the country, the Baganda kabaka, Frederick Mutesa III, was appointed president and the people were granted a certain amount of autonomy. During the 1970s, the infamous military dictator Idi Amin, a Baganda, ruled Uganda with an iron fist and ordered the deaths of hundreds of thousands of Ugandans in order to maintain control of the country. Under the new government of Yoweri Museveni, the Baganda are no longer as influential as they once were, but many hold jobs in the civil service sector.

Today, the Baganda make up 20 percent of the Uganda population and are divided into 36 clans, each named for an animal or plant. The basic social unit is the family, rather than the village, because each family is able to grow enough food to support itself. Houses in a Baganda village are built with plenty of space separating one from the other, with areas for growing plants and trees, such as bananas, in between. The traditional Baganda house is a thatched structure shaped like a large beehive. It is built by anchoring poles in the ground and layering thick-bladed grass over the poles to make the thatch walls, which eventually come to a point in the center at the top. Sometimes the interiors of Baganda houses are divided into several small rooms by bark-cloth drapes, which are also traditionally made by the Baganda. Pens for keeping sheep and sometimes cattle are built around each house. Also separate from the main house is the building for cooking.

The staple of the Baganda diet is the plantain, which may be eaten as fruit, made into a type of beer, or cooked. The Baganda also eat bananas, often as the main course combined with vegetables (such as sweet potatoes), fish, or chicken. Women traditionally used large earthenware pots for cooking, although aluminum pots are now used as well.

Both men and women farm. They grow plantains, potatoes, greens, beans, and bananas for their own use, and bananas, coffee, and cotton for export. Those men who live near the shores of Lake Victoria also catch fish to supplement their diet. Baganda men are accomplished engineers who build bridges, decorate buildings, and construct roads. They are also skilled at canoe building, pottery making, ironwork, and basketry. Whereas the traditional Baganda clothing was made of bark cloth and animal skins, men and women now wear cotton dresses and pants.

The Baganda have a rich tradition of oral literature in the form of songs and stories relating the history of the people. They are also known for their music—drums, harps, fifes—and for the dances that accompany the music. In many Baganda villages, the inhabitants get together for a nightly dance.

Religion has traditionally held great importance for the Baganda. As a result of their experience with British rule, the majority have adopted Christian beliefs. Some 15 percent are Muslim. Like many other African peoples, the Baganda originally worshipped the spirits of their ancestors as well as gods important to both the entire Baganda culture and to particular clans. Some Baganda still hold to those beliefs, along with newer Christian or Muslim ones.

While tradition dies hard, the Baganda are finding it necessary to adapt to the modern world. The primary reason is that their dependence on agriculture, which traditionally allowed them to be independent, has not prepared them well for the 20th-century African economy. When world prices for coffee, their main export, drop, so does their standard of living. Prices for coffee have been very unstable lately, and consequently the Baganda, while they have seldom experienced hunger, have been among the poorest people in Africa in recent years.

The Baganda are adapting to a changing world. The position of women is much stronger than it was about 40 years ago, when they were considered the property of men and had few rights. And 40 percent of the Baganda children who live in large cities such as Kampala, the capital, attend primary schools, but most of those who reside in the rural areas get no formal schooling. The traditional Baganda six-month calendar is being converted to the 12-month calendar used by most of the rest of the world. The Baganda are also making efforts to acquire modern technology so they will not be so dependent on agriculture in the future.

BAGGARA
(ba 'ga ra)

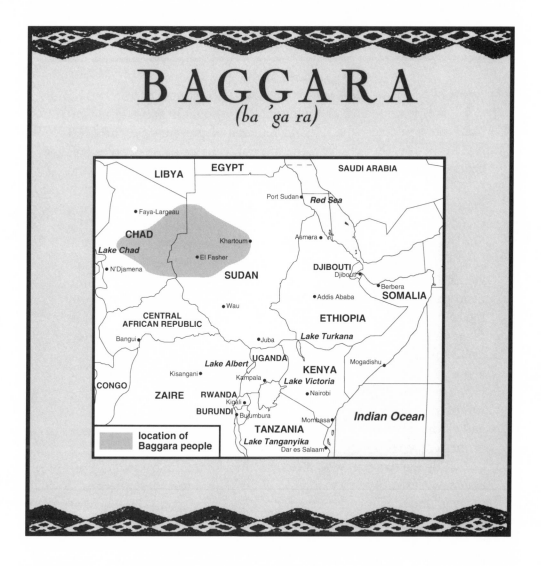

POPULATION:	5,000,000
LOCATION:	Sudan and Chad between the Nile River and Lake Chad
LANGUAGE:	Arabic
PRIMARY FOODS:	Milk, cheese, millet, goat, mutton

THE NOMADIC BAGGARA, WHOSE NAME MEANS "COW" IN ARABIC, are descendants of migrating Arab nomads and the indige- nous peoples who lived in the area of present-day Chad and Sudan. By the 18th century, the intermingling of these peoples had produced the Baggara. From their Arab ancestors, they retained the nomadic way of life, living in tents, traveling by camel, and conduct- ing raids on other peoples to obtain a supply of slave labor. From their African ancestors, they retained the agricultural practices of the Sudanic farmers and kin-based system of society.

The climate of the Baggara territory ranges from semiarid sa- vanna to moist grassland. The White Nile and its tributaries are the main geographical features. Although there are long dry seasons in the central and northern areas, the fertile slopes of the Jabal Marrah range in the western part are good for agriculture and grazing be- cause the climate is hot and humid and average rainfall is 60 inches a year.

The nomadic Baggara construct tent dwellings suitable to their way of life. The tents have wooden frames covered with animal skins and cloth woven of wool sheared from sheep or camels. The shape of the tents may vary. Although provided by the men, the tents are owned by the women, who also own the children in marriage. Fur- nishings consist of beds made of palm ribs tied together, a few sad- dlebags and decorated skins for storage, and goatskin bags for storing milk and water. A small wooden building called a *tukul* is constructed in each camp to serve as the communal kitchen.

Labor is divided between men and women according to tradi- tion. Women are responsible for the care of the household, milking the goats and cattle, looking after the children, and teaching the daughters to perform these duties. They also plant and harvest crops of millet, sorghum, and sesame. Men herd and tend the livestock, which includes camels, goats, sheep, and cattle kept in a thornbrush pen called a *zeriba*. Cattle, the most highly prized livestock, are a measure of wealth and prestige. The men also teach their sons these duties, and the sons assist them during the annual migration.

The Baggara today still practice retaliation as a way of righting wrongs and demand reparations or "blood money" from those who have harmed their people in any way. Baggara men carry daggers and rifles. Baggara warriors, using long spears called *kibis,* hunt elephants and hippopotamuses. Carrying their bows and arrows in a sack called a *turkash,* they hunt gazelles and small animals. From the early 1700s to the early 1900s, they made a practice of raiding other peoples' land for slaves, but the Baggara no longer practice slavery. Descendants of former slaves have been absorbed into the society as servants who assist with the crops and cattle.

The Baggara's diet consists mainly of milk and milk products. They also eat *umm duffan,* an unleavened bread made from the flour of ground millet. Often served with this bread is a sauce of butter with onions and spices. Sometimes meat is eaten, such as roasted goat or mutton stew or a goat's head that has been buried in ashes and baked overnight. Foods that the Baggara do not produce themselves, such as sugar and spices, are obtained by trading at markets. The traditional beverage is tea prepared in a large kettle, mixed with lots of sugar, and brewed all day. The consumption of alcohol is forbidden by the Baggara's Muslim faith.

The clothing of the Baggara is designed as a protection against the risk of malaria, which is at its height during the rainy season when mosquitoes breed in pools of water. To ward off insects, the people keep well covered. The men wear knee-length robes called *jibbas,* which are worn over pants. They cover their heads with headdresses made of strips of cotton cloth. They also wear cowskin sandals and wooden beads around their necks.

The traditional women's garb is a length of coarse blue cloth wrapped over a flowery cotton dress. A corner of the cloth may be pulled over the head. Women also wear amber necklaces, gold and ivory bracelets, rings, nose jewelry, and chains of silver around their ankles. They wear their hair long and in many braids and treat it with butter to make it shine.

Most Baggara do not read or write. Those who are literate are usually religious men who have studied the Koran, the Muslim holy book. But the Baggara maintain a highly developed oral tradition of storytelling. Conversation and storytelling are greatly valued because of the isolated existence of nomadic life. Stories may spring from the events of everyday life. Most often, however, they are concerned with fights or raids on other peoples. Stories are continually embellished and may eventually reach epic proportions.

Singing is also important to the Baggara, who compose songs

in a style borrowed from the Arabs of the north. As they watch over the grazing livestock, the young boys sing a special, four-line verse called a *dobbayt.* This rhyming song is usually about hunting, racing, or beautiful young girls. To accompany their songs, the Baggara make stringed instruments and drums from animal skins stretched over wooden or metal cylinders. Other traditional Baggara crafts include weaving, and making leather sandals, bags, and hassocks.

The Baggara today live much as their ancestors did, remaining a nomadic people who are continually searching for new grazing land. The Baggara have no broad political organization. They are broken up into small units led by a sheik who is chosen on the basis of descent through the father's line. Extended families are also patrilineal in descent, and to preserve the lineage, cousins are often preferred marriage partners. Family and personal lives are governed by the Islamic faith and local customs.

BEMBA
('behm bah)

| location of Bemba people | |

POPULATION:	150,000
LOCATION:	Zaire, Zambia, Zimbabwe
LANGUAGES:	Bemba, English
PRIMARY FOODS:	Millet, rice, soybeans, maize, meats

AN AGRICULTURAL SOCIETY THAT IN RECENT YEARS HAS BECOME almost entirely Westernized, the Bemba live primarily in the Great Rift Valley of Zambia. Some of the Bemba also live in eastern Zaire and northern Zimbabwe. Along with savannas, mountain ranges, and many lakes and rivers, the land is rich in copper deposits.

Compared with other African cultures, the Bemba is a relatively recent one; the Bemba kingdom was established around the 17th century. Their ancestors migrated from what is now southern Zaire and organized a series of villages of hunters and farmers. During the 18th and 19th centuries, the Bemba were powerful warriors who raided nearby kingdoms and captured villagers who were then sold as slaves. They also traded in ivory and copper.

When the slave trade came to an end in the late 1800s, many of the Bemba chiefs lost their political power. In the early 1900s, many of the Bemba were forced by the British to work in the copper mines, and during World War II they served in the British military. Following the war, the majority of the Bemba went to work as migrant laborers, and by the 1950s they were the largest labor group in Zambia. In 1961 the Bemba peacefully fought for majority rule, and in 1964 they gained their independence from the British.

Bemba wooden mask from the lower Congo area.

Carved motif from Bemba wooden mask.

Although prosperity from the copper mines has created an urban way of life for most of the Bemba, many still follow the traditional agricultural lifestyle. Modern farming has become more common, but the old *chitimene* system of slash-and-burn agriculture is still practiced. This system effectively enriches the soil, enabling the Bemba to produce enough crops for their survival. In addition to farming, many of the more traditional Bemba work in the copper mines. Their goal, however, is to work in the mines just long enough to save enough money in order to return to their villages.

Carved motifs from Bemba wooden sculpture.

The Bemba who reside in cities have brick houses, while those who still live in rural villages have dome-shaped homes made of branches and mud. The tradition of men taking more than one wife is dying out, as are many other old customs. Although some religious customs such as the worship of ancestor spirits are still practiced, most of the Bemba today consider themselves Christians. The Bemba style of dress, once dominated by dark cloth, is now almost entirely Western. Most of the Bemba currently work outside the home, buy food from urban markets, and follow many Western customs. In larger cities such as Mbala in Zambia, some Bemba children attend primary schools where classes are conducted in English. Also in Mbala is the Moto Moto Museum, which houses a fascinating collection of artifacts relating to Bemba history and culture. In Zambia, the Bemba society has for the most part become one with the national identity of the country.

CHOKWE
('choh kway)

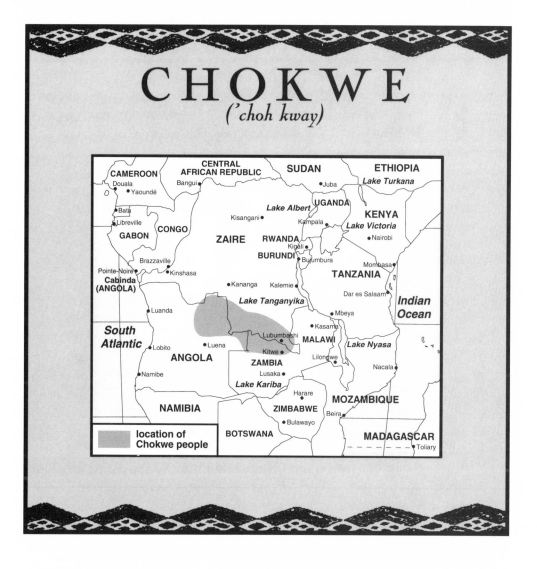

location of Chokwe people

POPULATION:	1,300,000
LOCATION:	Angola, Zambia, Zaire
LANGUAGES:	Chokwe (a Bantu language), Portuguese
PRIMARY FOODS:	Manioc, peanuts, yams, millet, beans, some beef and game

T HE CHOKWE PEOPLE SETTLED ALONG THE BORDERS OF ZAIRE, Zambia, and northeastern Angola. Primarily a high plateau region lying just south of the equator, it is an area of savanna grasslands and forest. From May to October, the weather is cool and dry, followed by a warm, rainy season from November to April. Several rivers cross the plateau from north to south, and over the centuries they have cut into the land to create rolling hills. Some of the land is good for agriculture because of fertile soil and adequate rainfall, and it is in these areas that the Chokwe settled as farmers and herders.

At one time, the Chokwe were part of the Lunda kingdom, and their legend of origin is that they are descended from the disinherited sons of a Lunda king. The sons moved westward, away from the kingdom, conquering other peoples along their way until A.D. 1600, when they established themselves as the Chokwe. Though geographically distant from the Lunda kingdom, the Chokwe continued to pay tribute to the Lunda chiefs until the late 1800s.

In the central plateau of what is now Angola, they met the Ovimbundu people, who had a thriving economy as middlemen between Portuguese slave traders and the native Africans of central Africa. The Chokwe joined the Ovimbundu in providing slaves for sale to the Portuguese. In fact, the plateau region became a principal area in the slave trade, and throughout the early 1800s slaves continued to be captured here and shipped to Brazil. As a result of this long-term export of slaves, the plateau region became one of the most sparsely populated areas of Africa.

During the mid- to late 1800s, trading expanded to include ivory, wax, food, and rubber. By trading these goods, as well as slaves, for firearms, the Chokwe were able to conquer neighboring cultures and expand their territory. By 1890 they had reached the height of their power, at which time the European colonizers of Africa attempted to subdue them. The Chokwe resisted and eventually laid claim to the territory they now occupy. Today, they continue to resist outside influence and retain much of their traditional lifestyle.

The Chokwe, who have never been united under a single ruler, are still very scattered with no unifying political structure. The majority live in small villages and towns, some of which are self-ruled,

A traveling Chokwe entertainer from Zaire wears a mask representing the female spirit, *Mwana Pwo*.

Chokwe decorated wooden comb.

others of which are part of chiefdoms. Few of these towns have a population of more than 2,000. The Chokwe construct their houses of branch frames covered with leaves and sod. The houses are built in circular and square shapes and are laid out in a circle around a central meeting house.

Chokwe wooden mask.

The carved pattern on a Chokwe wooden musical
instrument called a "bush piano."

Although they are primarily farmers and cattle herders, the
Chokwe still hunt game, a reflection of their past as great hunters of
elephants for their ivory tusks. The women do most of the farming—
cultivating manioc, yams, beans, peanuts, maize, and millet—and
also do the cooking. During the dry season, the men hunt. They also
sell goods or their own crops to earn money for such things as salt
and kerosene and their children's school tuition.

Family relationships are highly structured. A newly married
couple will go to live in the village of the groom's mother's brothers.
The wife must behave in a very formal manner in the presence of
her in-laws. In fact, she may not eat out of the same dish or even in
the same room as they. With her own kin, she can enjoy a much
more casual relationship.

Chokwe clothing is still very traditional. The women wear long
wraparound skirts with blouses and sometimes a shawl or blanket as
well. To transport buckets of water or bundles of wood, a woman
will fashion a carrying platform out of cloth wrapped around her
head. Hair is usually worn in braids and fastened with ivory or bone
ornaments. Massive necklaces of wood, metal, or stone are the most
striking aspect of the Chokwe woman's attire. Both men and women
wear numerous bracelets of copper or tin on their forearms.

Although the men may wear Western-style pants and shirts,
they also continue to wear the more traditional length of cloth
wrapped at the waist and extending to midcalf. In cooler weather,
heavy blankets are used instead of cloth.

Although some of the best Chokwe crafts were produced before 1860, the Chokwe are still known for their craftsmanship. They
sculpt very realistic figurines of their ancestors, as well as abstract
animals. They are famous, too, for their carved wooden masks and

carvings in ivory and bone. Other craft items include baskets and metal jewelry.

Chokwe history is preserved in their tradition of storytelling. Experiences of the past are shared to provide an understanding of the Chokwe way of life. Stories, which are called *yishima,* are sometimes even used in court to settle disputes. They serve to entertain as well as to educate, and the good storyteller is so skillful that he can cause the audience to interact with the characters in the tale.

Chokwe religion is based on an all-powerful being who created the world but who is not concerned with the actions of people on earth. Nature spirits and ancestors are the guardians of the world, and each village has a central sacred ground reserved for their worship. The Chokwe bring offerings of clay figures and food for their ancestors. When illness or death occurs, it is believed to be a result of human sorcery. (The Chokwe have an average life span of under 45 years, so this belief is understandable.)

Years of civil strife in Angola and government restrictions on agriculture have contributed to the poverty and short life span of the Chokwe. But their refusal to adhere to a national government has been a factor as well.

DINKA
('deen kuh)

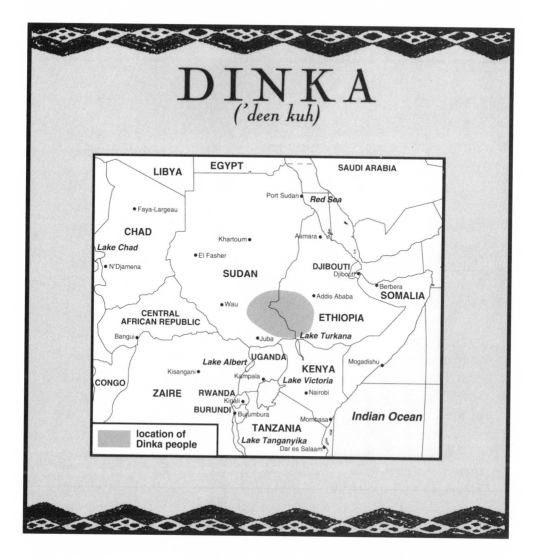

location of
Dinka people

POPULATION:	1,000,000
LOCATION:	Sudan and Ethiopia
LANGUAGE:	Dinka
PRIMARY FOODS:	Sour milk, fresh blood, sorghum porridge, grain, beans, fish

T HE TERRITORY OCCUPIED BY THE DINKA IS IN A PLAIN SHARED BY southeast Sudan and southwest Ethiopia. An enormous swamp—the largest on earth—is located at the edge of this dry, sandy plain where it approaches the Sudd. The swamp gives way to dense tropical forest dotted with lagoons and marsh pools. Vegetation produces a damlike situation, blocking the flow of the White Nile and flooding the plain for thousands of square miles. Three other rivers feed the area as well: on the south, the Bor River; on the west, the Aweil River; and on the north, the Renk River. The climate is hot and humid, with rainfall of 30–60 inches per year. During the dry season, the banks of the White Nile attract grazing cattle.

Around 3,000 B.C., herders who also fished and grew some crops settled in the area. The Dinka are one of the three groups who were eventually formed out of these original settlers in the Nile region. Dinka society began to spread throughout the region between A.D. 1500 and 1800. They were fighters who resisted the incursions of the Ottoman Turks in the middle 1800s, as well as attempts by slave merchants to convert them to the Muslim faith.

The social organization of the Dinka is egalitarian, which means there is no class system. While some Dinka may be wealthier than others, all are expected to contribute to the community. Each village is occupied by one or more extended families, and every Dinka must know his or her ancestors, because there are strict taboos against marriage to someone in your own family.

The leader or village chief is expected to serve the good of the entire village through reason and persuasion. The most influential leaders are called Chiefs of the Fishing Spear, which is the Dinka symbol of authority and responsibility. The Dinka reject external forms of authority based on their past experience with outside rulers who have tried to dominate them with force. Instead, they value discussing and resolving problems in public and pursue a lifestyle based on honor and dignity. All Dinka are expected to be kind and generous to others in order to achieve status within their own culture.

The Dinka build their permanent villages on the higher, dry ground of the savanna and live in these villages during the rainy

A Dinka subchief from Sudan with horizontal scarification on his forehead, 1947.

season. Houses are constructed of dried mud and wattle—a combination of branches and reeds—and topped with a cone-shaped roof. Each house also has a wooden platform inside, raised on stilts and enclosed with dried mud walls to protect against moisture. Only women and children sleep inside; men sleep outside in mud-roofed

A Dinka village on the Upper Nile, 1931.

pens with their cattle. Cooking is also done outdoors in pots over hearths built of stone.

Besides their homes in the villages, the Dinka build temporary shelters along the riverbanks during the dry season. These huts are low to the ground and igloo shaped. They are formed out of saplings that are bent to make the frame and then covered with dried grass.

Cattle are a symbol of wealth to the Dinka, and this importance is reflected in their customs. A young boy is given his first ox at puberty. The boy forms an attachment to the ox and cares for it, grooming and spending much time with the animal. He even composes a song to his ox, and thus a boy's first ox is called his *song ox.*

Dinka cattle are generally not killed for food or used to carry loads and work the land. They are regarded as valuable possessions and are watched over at all times. They are slaughtered and eaten only after being sacrificed in religious ceremonies or when they have reached extreme old age.

Family life also reflects the importance of cattle. A young man must pay a bride-price of cattle to the family of his bride. This practice, called *bridewealth,* makes daughters a valuable resource for families. A wealthy Dinka man may take as many brides as he can afford.

Men of the Dinka usually wear either a loincloth or a *jellaba,* which is a full-length Arab-style tunic. Women wear loose cotton wraps tied at one shoulder. On festive occasions, elaborate vests of multicolored beads are worn. Dinka wear very little clothing within the confines of the village, and this is especially true for young children. Despite these traditions, Western-style clothing is finding its way into the Dinka wardrobe.

Personal grooming is important. The Dinka rub their skins with oil from boiled butter or from the seeds of the shea tree. Dung ash is worn to repel mosquitoes, and faces and bodies are decorated with ornamental painting. Dinka also beautify their bodies with patterns of flowers or abstract designs, cut into the skin with sharp instruments in a practice called *scarification.* Another beauty rite is the removal of a few teeth. Men dye their hair red with cow urine; women shave their eyebrows and heads, leaving only a knot of hair on the very top of the skull. Men and women adorn themselves with feathers, bead necklaces, earrings, rings, and brass or ivory bracelets and leg bands.

The Dinka are skilled at a variety of crafts. Women make pottery and weave baskets and papyrus mats. Men are expert blacksmiths, making metal items such as spears, hammers, cooking utensils, and farm tools.

Poetic language and song are important elements of Dinka culture. Songs serve many purposes in their lives: they are sung in courtship and to prepare the bride for marriage; they are performed during ritual ceremonies such as the scarring of a young boy's forehead, and to transmit legends to succeeding generations. They also provide an outlet for the expression of feelings, pleas, insults, or accusations that might otherwise be taken as offensive. Popular songs often move their listeners to take some form of action.

Although the Dinka have retained much of their independence and continue to be mostly self-governing, many of them now enjoy the benefits of the modern world. Some have taken advantage of the national educational laws that enable them to attend schools with the English-speaking peoples in their countries, and many others have adopted Western-style dress and habits.

DOGON

(doe gun)

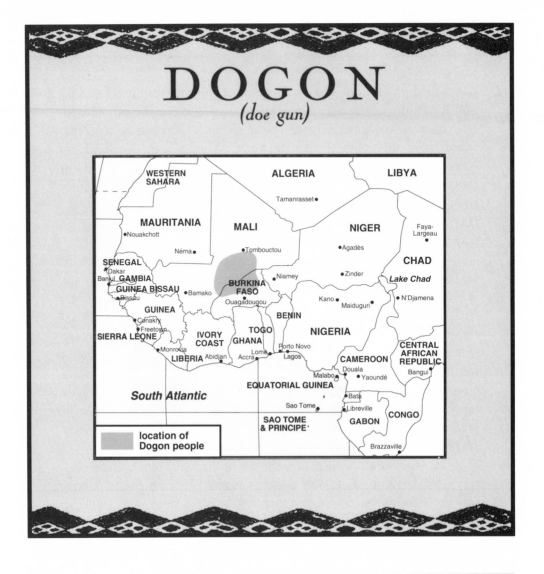

location of
Dogon people

POPULATION:	250,000
LOCATION:	Southern Mali and northern Burkina Faso
LANGUAGE:	Dogon
PRIMARY FOODS:	Grains, some meat, fish

THE DOGON, WHOSE ARTIFACTS HAVE BEEN DATED AS FAR BACK AS 500 B.C., are among the oldest African cultures. During the fifth century B.C., they migrated to the mountains south of the Great Niger Bend, drove out the resident Tellem peoples, and then settled in the area around Bandiagara to farm on the arid, rocky plateau. Throughout their existence, they have been repeatedly threatened by more powerful neighbors—the Songhai to the north, the Hausa to the east, and the Mande to the west. The need to resist these outside forces, it has been suggested, led to their creation of what is perhaps the most ordered way of life among African peoples. The basis for this way of life is a collection of myths that explain the structure of the universe and how the Dogon fit into that structure. Their steadfast belief in these myths is one of the reasons that the Dogon have held on to their ancient traditions longer than most other African societies.

Almost everything in Dogon life is systemized, from the layout of fields and villages to politics and the roles of the two sexes. The Dogon are mainly farmers, and the proper arrangement of fields is centered around three ritual fields, which are laid out in the shape of a square. The fields for regular cultivation are laid out along the four sides of that square. This concept of ritual fields is tied to the Dogon mythology whereby all aspects of life must be in proper alignment with what they believe to be the structure of the universe. There is even a special way to clear these fields. The farmer must turn his back on the field already cleared, and the front edge of each new field should be longer than the back to represent the opening up of the universe.

Each extended family should have eight fields, grouped in pairs on each side of the square. Each field is cultivated in a zigzag pattern, and with each step the farmer must move the hoe from the right hand to the left hand. Each patch of land should have eight lines of grain, and each line of grain should be eight feet long.

Until about 300 years ago, Dogon villages were built near high sandstone cliffs for protection. The ideal Dogon village is at the center of a field and is laid out to represent the human body. A blacksmith's shop stands at one end (the head); then there is the

A Dogon woman carrying her child on her back, from the Sanga region in Mali.

group of family homes (the body); and a cone-shaped shrine representing fertility is at the other end. Houses for menstruating women
are located off to the sides like arms.

Individual houses are also built to represent the body. The
kitchen at the north end is the head, the two hearths are the eyes,

Dolo, a Dogon blacksmith/wood carver and his 14-year-old son, Samuel, cut softwood trees to make a Kanaga mask, Ogol du Haut, Mali.

and two lines of storerooms on each side are the arms. The stable is at the south end, and the towers at the ends and either side of the stable are the hands and feet.

Dogon men are responsible for hunting, fishing, and looking after livestock. Both sexes clear the fields and plant and harvest the crops. Dogon women take the surplus produce to market and are responsible for cooking and child care as well as for gathering fresh water and firewood.

Both men and women do work such as pottery, weaving, and basketry. According to Dogon tradition, pottery was the first craft taught to their ancestors by their creator-god, Amma. Weaving is among the most revered crafts, and the skill of the Dogon in making

Dolo making the Kanaga mask.

woven tunics and caps is widely known. Both sexes wear colorful clothing (cotton dresses for women and tunics for men) as well as some sort of headgear (tied scarves for women—to help carry loads of produce on their heads—and skullcaps for men). Women wear necklaces of beads and metal medallions.

Perhaps the most highly prized craft of the Dogon is wood carving. Traditionally, the doors and beams of granaries and houses

Dolo and Samuel position the crosspieces on the Kanaga mask.

were decorated with elaborate carvings, but Dogon carvings have been so sought after by anthropologists and collectors that few of the original carvings remain. Dogon wood-carvers also make masks, which are used during rituals and celebration dances.

Because funeral ceremonies are among the most important, funeral masks have great significance. Such masks are used at funerals to give the spirits of the dead a new place to live and prevent them from harming those still living while they are searching for a new body. Often, men dress in tall, elaborate masks, brightly colored straw skirts, and vestlike constructions of shells.

The most important mask of all is called *Iminana,* the Great Mask. It commemorates the original ancestors of the Dogon and is used primarily for the funeral rites of high-ranking members of the community. It is shaped like a serpent with a rectangular head. The body of the serpent is sometimes very long, making it a challenge for the wearer to balance the mask. Only the most skilled and respected carver makes a Great Mask, for it is expected to last 60

Bird design carved on a Dogon wooden door from Mali.

Profile of a Dogon wooden sculpture from Mali.

years, after which a new mask will be carved and presented to the community in a ceremony called *Sigui.*

Other masks are of animal and bird figures. The most frequently used mask is the *Kanaga* mask, representing the bird of the same name. The kanaga is a mask of atonement that protects the wearer from the revenge of a killed animal. A number of masks represent human characteristics, such as old age or deafness.

Strong religious belief goes into the carving of these masks, but in the past 30 years some of the Dogon have begun producing masks for the tourist art market. Although the average tourist purchasing one of these masks would likely not notice a difference, art historians can easily distinguish between authentic masks produced for the Dogon themselves and those that are carved with haste for the tourist market.

Like other aspects of life, the Dogon's religious system is highly complex and ordered, with detailed creation stories and a great variety of myths to explain different parts of the universe. They involve the creator-god, Amma, who made the earth from a lump of clay, and eight ancestors, pairs of whom came to earth and founded the four Dogon groups, the Arou, Dyon, Ono, and the Domnu. Throughout these myths, there is a sense of balance between masculine and feminine, earth and sky, physical and spiritual.

EWE

('e vay)

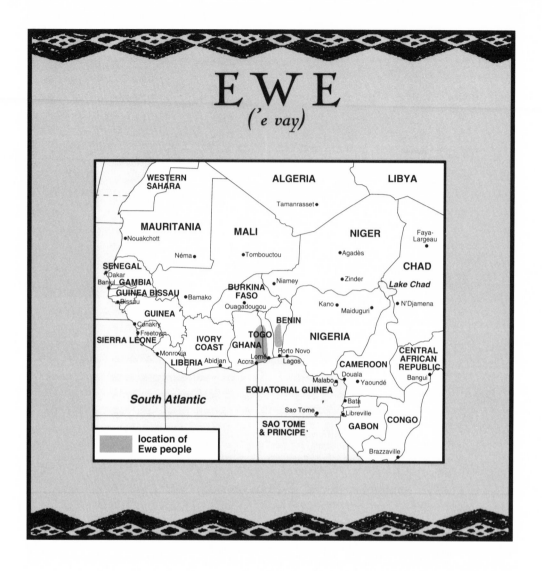

location of
Ewe people

POPULATION:	700,000
LOCATION:	Togo, Ghana, Benin
LANGUAGE:	Ewe
PRIMARY FOODS:	Yams, corn, millet, plantains, vegetables, peppers

THE EWE PEOPLE LIVE ALONG A NARROW STRIP OF LAND ABOUT 80 miles wide and 400 miles long on the west coast of Africa. The area is divided by the Ghana-Togo border and has three distinct physical zones. Bounded by the Gulf of Guinea is a densely populated southern coastal area. Beyond lies a grassy savanna. To the north and in the interior are a sandstone plateau and an upland forest region.

During a period of drought and famine in the 12th century, pre-Ewe peoples are thought to have joined with the Yoruba in migrating to a town called Ketou, located in what would now be Benin. Further migration occurred in the 13th century, probably due to overpopulation, and the migrating people split into two groups during the westward movement. One group founded the settlement of Tado on the Mono River. A subgroup of this settlement split off and migrated to the plateau region. Another subgroup, which moved eastward and founded the Adja kingdom of Alladah, are believed to be the ancestors of the Anglo-Ewe. They settled in the walled town of Nuatja, living peacefully with several different peoples, each with their own chief, but all unified under one king.

This unity was shattered around the middle of the 17th century under King Agolkoli, a brutal ruler who practiced human sacrifice. Many people fled Nuatja to escape this cruelty. One group settled in the coastal lagoon area, another group settled in the uplands, and a middle group settled near the Togo mountains in the plateau region. Throughout this migration and subdividing, the Ewe preserved a loose alliance of clans and large extended families that managed to keep the culture intact.

In the meantime, European interest in the slave trade had heightened, and slaves had begun to surpass gold as the main African export. European slave traders dealt with the more powerful coastal and inland peoples, including the Ashanti, the Akwamu, and the Akyema. These groups in turn preyed on the weaker groups of the inland regions for their source of slaves. In the 1700s the Ashanti, in the course of their wars of expansion, conquered several other cultures, one of which, the Akwamu, was driven into Ewe territory and subsequently captured thousands of Ewe people.

The Ewe were forced to pay tribute to their conquerors in the form of goods and slaves. This domination by the Akwamu lasted

A 1989 Ewe festival in Notse, Togo.

nearly 100 years, until the Ewe fought for and won their independence. But the years of domination and strife had nearly destroyed
the Ewe and their territory.

After the Ewe assisted the British in subduing the Ashanti, the
British moved in and established colonial rule in the 1800s. In a
very short time, however, the British turned the territory over to the
Germans as part of the pact made in 1899. Under the Germans, the
Ewe pursued growth and development in several areas, including
the creation of a cash-crop economy, a system of roads, a missionary
education system, and a railway. But many Ewe still chafed under
foreign rule and migrated to the Gold Coast before World War I.
After the war, their country was divided into three territories: French
Togoland, British Togoland, and the Gold Coast. Not until 1951,
under the leadership of Sylvanus Olympio, was a real push for Ewe
reunification begun.

The British were the first to agree to unify British Togoland
with the Gold Coast. By 1960, following elections supervised by the
United Nations, French Togoland became the Republic of Togo,

with Olympio as its first president. Under his leadership, Togo flourished, growing from a dependent state to a self-sufficient nation.

In large cities such as Lomé in Togo, most of the Ewe live in run-down apartments where urban poverty is the norm. The Ewe who reside in rural areas are farmers who live in compounds of extended families and who generally have better living conditions than those who dwell in cities. Since the social order of the Ewe is determined by lineage, the inhabitants of a village can trace their descent to a common male ancestor. Each town, or *frome*, is headed by a chieftan who is responsible for the spiritual and social life of the community. Land belongs to the men.

Each mud-clay house in the town has its own yard opening onto a courtyard shared by everyone in the compound. An Ewe man may have more than one wife, but each wife, along with her children, must be given a separate house within the compound. The husband, too, must have his own house.

The men of the village grow the crops, which usually consist of maize, millet, yams, beans, cassava, and peanuts. The main cash crop today is cocoa. The land is cultivated by hand after being cleared by burning. The crops are grown for both food and trade, and it is the women who handle the trading in the marketplace. In the coastal areas, the Ewe subsist by fishing rather than farming.

Families have garden plots cared for by the women, whose duties also include caring for the children and cooking. The main dish prepared by Ewe women is *fufu,* which is made from yams that have been peeled, boiled, and pounded, and then served in a sauce made of oil and hot peppers. Dried fish is sometimes eaten, but meat and eggs are scarce. *Sodabe,* a homemade palm wine, and fermented millet beer are traditional to the Ewe diet.

Both men and women dress in a *pagne,* a large square of cotton cloth wrapped at the waist. In the cities, some men wear shorts and T-shirts, while the women may wear a blouse or a camisole with their pagne.

The Ewe engage in a wide variety of crafts, among them pottery, weaving, basketry, wood carving, and blacksmithing. The men are famous for their carved and sculpted wooden stools and drums. The women weave not only baskets but also mats for sleeping and kitchen use, for the home, and for sale.

Although the Ewe were converted to Christianity by European missionaries, many still worship a high god called Mawu (the all-wise creator and giver of good things). Like many other African cultures, they believe in ancestor worship, which is reflected in the importance of the ancestral stool that each family line keeps and worships. The Ewe also believe that certain people have supernatural powers and are capable of causing harm, illness, and even death to others. To ward off this sorcery, or rectify it if it does occur, many Ewe hire the services of an *afakaka,* or soothsayer, who uses herbal medicines and special prayers as antidotes.

Today, the Ewe remain divided by the national politics of Ghana, Togo, and Benin. In Togo they are the largest ethnic group, representing about 35 percent of the population. In Benin they are a small minority. Because of the unstable market in cocoa, and years of political conflicts in all three countries, most of the Ewe live in poverty. A few hold government jobs in urban centers, but most still adhere to their traditional farming lifestyle.

FALASHA
(fah 'lah shaw)

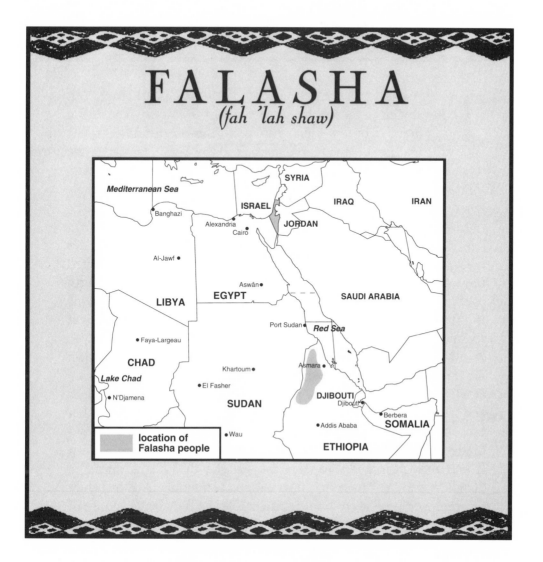

POPULATION:	25,000
LOCATION:	Northern Ethiopia, Israel
LANGUAGES:	Amharic, Tigrinya, Ge'ez
PRIMARY FOODS:	Dairy products, grains, fruit, chicken, goat, hot peppers

THE BLACK JEWS OF ETHIOPIA, THE FALASHA LIVE IN THE SIMEN Mountains in the northwest section of the country. The region is bounded by the Tekeze River to the north and east, the Blue Nile and Lake Tana to the south, and the Sudan border to the west. The rugged land is dotted with scrub bushes and has a rocky topsoil not well suited for farming. Unlike other areas of Ethiopia where torrential rains cause serious flooding, the land of the Falasha receives only moderate showers.

According to an ancient legend, the history of the Falasha dates back to biblical times when the Ethiopian queen of Sheba visited the Jewish king Solomon, and after returning to Ethiopia gave birth to their son, Menelik. Years later, Menelik founded a Jewish colony in Ethiopia. Another Falasha legend claims that the tribe was founded when Moses married an Ethiopian princess.

More modern records note that the Falasha created their own nation in Ethiopia during the 13th century. In the following two centuries, Christian groups repeatedly tried to conquer the Falasha and eventually established an Ethiopian Christian kingdom that eroded the unity of the people. By the 1600s, the Falasha were forbidden from owning land and subjected to persecution and slavery. It was the Christians who gave the Falasha their name, meaning "landless people." Although this name is commonly used in Ethiopia, the people prefer to refer to themselves as Beta Israel (house of Israel). At one time the Falasha consisted of about 150,000 people, but years of subjugation led to a drastic decline in the population.

During the 18th and 19th centuries, tens of thousands of Falasha were sold into slavery in an effort to aid the failing Ethiopian economy. When European missionaries brought back to Europe the news of what had happened to the Falasha, European Jews came to their aid. In the early 1900s, European Jews established schools in Ethiopia for the Falasha, and by the 1950s an exchange program was created that enabled the Falasha to study in Israel. By the 1970s, many of the Falasha tried to emigrate to the "promised land" of Israel, making the long journey by camel and on foot. Political unrest and severe famine in Ethiopia increased their desire to leave. In the mid-1980s, the Israeli government established "Operation Moses," an airlift that brought over 8,000 Falasha to Israel.

Today about half of the Falasha population resides in Israel,

Falasha women display their needlework.

where they have made the slow transition from living in settlement camps to becoming assimilated into Israeli society. Most of those who live in Ethiopia are burdened by droughts, malnutrition, malaria, tuberculosis, and dysentery. A few who reside in Ethiopian cities have slightly better living conditions working as shopkeepers and clerks.

Falasha villages in Ethiopia are usually perched on a hill with a river nearby. Their small, round houses are constructed of mud and dung with cone-shaped roofs. Each village contains a rustic synagogue for religious services. Most of the villages cultivate cotton, sorghum, and sesame as cash crops; and wheat, vegetables, and beans for their own consumption. If they can afford it, families maintain a small corral for goats, chickens, and cattle.

The Falasha who live in Ethiopian villages wear the traditional Ethiopian white cotton toga known as a *shamma*. Women wear their

shammas over long dresses, and men wear them over pants. The
clothing of both men and women is often decorated with embroidered Jewish symbols such as the Star of David. It is customary for
the Falasha to go barefoot. Those living in Israel wear Western-style
clothing.

Falasha families are very close, and the family unit is considered
an important element in their lives. Duties of family life are dictated
by the Jewish religion and are equally divided between the sexes.
Men build the houses, work in the fields, and care for livestock;
women prepare meals, sew, and fetch water and firewood. Girls are
allowed to marry as early as the age of 12, and boys usually marry at
about the age of 18; wedding ceremonies are an elaborate affair
sometimes lasting up to eight days. The celebration begins at the
groom's family's home, where a priest wraps a string around the
groom's forehead. The entourage then proceeds to the bride's home
for the night, and the next day the bride is lifted in the air and
carried back to the groom's home for more celebrations.

Common foods of the Falasha include sour milk, yogurt, spicy
grain dishes, and vegetables. A flat, pancakelike bread called *injera*
accompanies most meals. A red pepper stew, called *wot,* makes for
a favorite evening meal. Meat and chicken are occasionally mixed
into the stew and added to bowls of grain. A fermented barley drink
similar to beer is consumed on special occasions. At family meals,
the oldest daughter serves the food to the parents first and then to
herself and siblings.

Like Orthodox Jews elsewhere, the Falasha follow strict religious customs based on the Torah and the Old Testament regarding
diet, cleanliness, prayers, festivals; and ceremonies of birth, death,
and marriage. On Saturdays, the Jewish Sabbath, all the Falasha
rest; no cooking or work-related activities are allowed. In preparation for the Sabbath, the Falasha wash themselves in a river as a
way of purifying themselves for the next day's rituals. Not all Jewish
customs, however, are observed. The Falasha celebrate the holy days
of Rosh Hashanah and Yom Kippur, but they do not observe Ha-
nukkah. And some of their religious practices reveal a hint of Christian influence: Instead of rabbis, they call their religious leaders
priests; and they regularly confess their sins to these priests.

Arts and crafts are an important part of Falasha life, dating back to the 17th century when they were forced to become craftsmen by the Christian rulers. Although their clay pottery, weaving, and metalwork have earned the Falasha income, Ethiopian society looks down on craftspeople because they are thought to represent bad luck. In addition to the crafts, the Falasha produce knives, tools, and axes.

The Falasha now living in Israel are undergoing a major process of adjustment to their new home. Along with learning to speak Hebrew, they must deal with the details of modern life such as electrical appliances, grocery stores, and banks. Although the process of assimilation has been difficult for both the Falasha and the Israelis, overall the future looks bright. For those Falasha still in Ethiopia, however, the prospects for the future are less promising.

FANG
(fang)

location of
Fang people

POPULATION:	1,000,000
LOCATION:	Southern Cameroon, eastern Equatorial Guinea, and northern Gabon
LANGUAGE:	Fang, a Bantu language
PRIMARY FOODS:	Meat, fish, grains, roots, plantains, yams, cassava

ACCORDING TO THE ORAL HISTORIES THE FANG HAVE PASSED down to recent generations, the people originally came from southern Cameroon and settled in the forested regions just north of the equator in eastern Equatorial Guinea and northern Gabon. When this occurred is uncertain, because the only documented history of the culture comes from the Europeans who first encountered them. Temperatures in the Fang region average 82 degrees Fahrenheit year-round, and abundant rainfall, between 60 and 100 inches a year, flows into the Atlantic Ocean by way of the Sanaga and Nyong rivers. The dense forests eventually open into grass- and shrubland near the equator.

The Fang evolved from various migrating peoples coming together in a central area. These migrations were preceded and accompanied by an extended period of trading by the Africans living along the west coast and various European traders beginning with the Portuguese in the 1470s. The ivory and slave trades soon attracted other European traders.

By 1807, settlements had been established by the Portuguese, British, French, and Dutch. During this period, a group of Africans who had migrated from the rain forests in the northern part of what is now Cameroon began to settle in the area near the European settlements. The Europeans were frightened of the native Africans because they had heard rumors that they practiced cannibalism and sorcery. The Fang, as they came to be known, quickly grew in size by absorbing the best warriors of the cultures they defeated, and by 1900 they were the largest society in the region.

Although they had once been farmers, after the arrival of Europeans the Fang turned to hunting elephants for ivory which they traded with other Africans, who in turn traded with the Europeans. Eventually, the Fang began trading directly with the Europeans and gained a reputation for their intelligence, language skills, strength, and fighting ability.

Fang leaders did not want their people to become economically dependent on the Europeans, so they discouraged interaction with the Europeans and limited trade to ivory and forest products. Unlike other African peoples, the Fang did not engage in the slave trade.

As times changed, so did the adaptable Fang. After World War I, when the African economy shifted from trading in ivory and forest

Small-mammal design carved on a Fang bone
counter from Gabon.

products to trading in farm goods, the Fang became farmers. When
the French began to take advantage of the timber resources in the
area where the Fang lived, however, the Fang were threatened by
French weaponry and forced to neglect their crops. Famine resulted,
along with an epidemic of influenza and smallpox that killed thousands of Fang during the 1930s.

In the 1940s, the French began to encourage local governments
and self-rule in Cameroon, and the Fang reorganized their villages
according to clan ties. This reorganization gave them a base of power

A Fang wooden guardian figure from Gabon.

Fang wooden sculpture from Gabon.

that they used, with other peoples, to gain the independence of
Gabon in 1960.

Today, many Fang live in cities or suburbs, and many own their
own coffee and cocoa plantations. Wealthy individuals live in Western-style houses. Those who reside in villages are more likely to farm
for their own food and not for export.

Fang villages are usually laid out in a linear fashion with houses
lining each side of the main street, and an *abeng,* or traveler's house,
at one end of the road. A simple community meeting house, constructed of wooden poles supporting a roof, is located in the central
square. The individual houses are built of wood or bamboo frames
with mud walls and two-sided thatched roofs. These houses are rectangular and divided into five rooms for cooking and sleeping.

Fang women do all the cooking, cleaning, and caring for the
children. They make the traditional *gari,* a thick porridge of insects
seasoned with spices. Meat usually comes from the men's hunting
expeditions, and fruits and vegetables are bought at a market. Millet
beer, palm wine, and banana-juice wine are traditional drinks. Although it would appear that the rural Fang eat a balanced diet, di-
etary taboos for pregnant women (no eggs, meat, or fruit) and poor
soil conditions have contributed to malnutrition among infants and
young children.

Men clear the land and do the farming and hunting. They also
make all decisions. In the male-centered Fang society, women may

cook only for their own households and may not engage in any activity that is not for their husbands.

Fang in rural areas still practice the tradition of decorating their bodies with tattoos and scarification. The tattoos are created by professionals who use a blue pigment from a local tree fungus. Scarification is done with a sharp instrument, such as a nail, followed by an herb ointment to prevent infection. In both rural and urban areas, Western-style clothing is the preferred garb among the Fang. Women may wear the traditional *pagne* cloth wrapped around their waist to form a skirt, topped by a tank top or blouse. Men wear trousers and shirts or business suits.

The Fang have a highly developed artistic tradition and produce paintings, sculpture, poetry, and songs accompanied by a string instrument called an *invet*. Wandering minstrels preserve the story of the Fang migration, and Fang unity is celebrated in the annual festival of *esooulan* with songs and a colorful dance called *enyengue*.

The original Fang religion was called *Bwiti*. Its central belief was that some people had special mystical powers that enabled them to do harm to others. To protect themselves from these people, the Fang sought the help of secret societies, who also had special powers, called *bieri*. In the 1800s, many Fang were converted to Christianity, but belief in these mystical powers and secret societies remains to this day, especially in the rural areas.

Today, many Fang hold government, administrative, and academic positions in Equatorial Guinea, where they are the largest ethnic group in the country and make up 80 percent of the population. In Gabon they represent 25 percent of the population, and many hold bureaucratic positions. In Cameroon the Fang are a small minority, but several have prominent government jobs. In all three countries many Fang are successful commercial farmers, and more than half of all Fang children attend primary schools.

FON
(fawn)

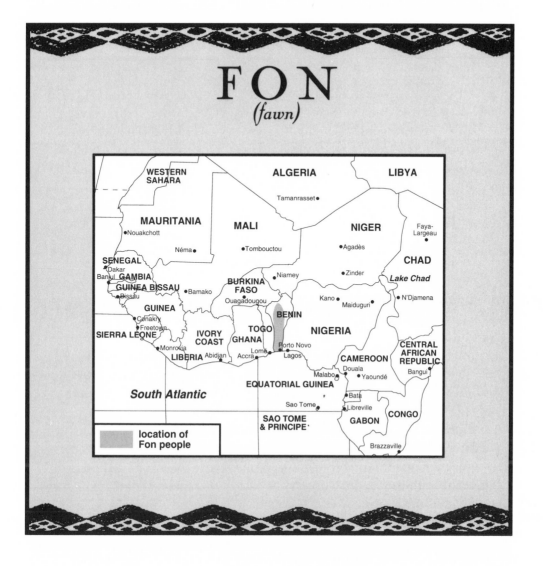

location of
Fon people

POPULATION:	1,000,000
LOCATION:	Benin
LANGUAGES:	Fon, French
PRIMARY FOODS:	Yams, corn, millet, okra, plantains, fish, poultry, meat, beer

ONCE A WARRIOR NATION THAT INCLUDED THE LEGENDARY female Amazon warriors, the Fon live in the central west African country of Benin, formerly called Dahomey. It is a hot and humid region where the average temperature ranges from 70 to almost 100 degrees. The country's primary river, the Ouémé, flows down from the northern mountains and empties into the Atlantic Ocean. Along the coast there are flat, sandy beaches, lagoons, and dense mangrove swamps. Heavy rains and monsoon winds are a nuisance here. North of the coastal region there are vast savannas, forests, and sandstone hills. Dry, dusty winds blow down from the Sahara Desert.

Most research suggests the Fon were once members of the Oyo Empire who migrated south from the Niger River because of famine and drought, and who settled in present-day Benin during the 13th century. During the 1500s, this group founded the Allada kingdom in southern Dahomey and prospered as slave traders. After a series of disputes among the royalty, a new Fon kingdom called Dahomey was established in 1625. This new kingdom grew quite aggressive, utilizing slave raids to increase its wealth and human sacrifices to calm angry spirit ancestors.

The kingdom established a large army that used guns acquired in trade with the Europeans. By the late 1700s the Fon had greatly expanded their territory and power by waging war on nearby kingdoms and controlling much of the region's slave trade. Owing to constant threats from the original Oyo peoples, the Fon bolstered their power in the area by adding female warriors to their army and created the legendary Amazon corps of Dahomey. These Amazons, equipped with uniforms and guns, made up one-third of the Fon army and fought alongside Fon men during violent raids against less powerful cultures.

In 1894, Dahomey was claimed by the French, and the Fon kingdom fell under their rule. Following World War II, the French set up an extensive education system in Dahomey, and many Fon went on to become artists, educators, writers, professionals, and government officials. Although France granted independence to the country in 1960, Dahomey continued to be plagued by rivalries between the Fon, Yoruba, and other peoples. In 1975 the country

Fon man making appliquéd cloth in Abomey, Benin.

Fon women perform the dance of the women warriors at the king's palace in Abomey, Benin.

changed its name to Benin, and many Fon now serve as administrators in the government. They also represent the largest ethnic group in the country.

Most of Benin's Fon now live in the rural areas of the coastal regions. Unfortunately the country suffers from a poor economy, and many of the Fon need government assistance to survive. Palm products are a mainstay of the economy, and palm farming provides jobs for some of the Fon. Others work in the shipping, cotton, coffee, or cocoa industries, and some Fon are farmers, raising yams, corn, manioc, and other vegetables for cash. Others raise poultry or work as fishermen. Many Fon hold positions as administrators in the national government.

The Fon social structure is patrilineal; land is inherited by children through the father. Marriages are usually arranged by the parents on both sides, and the bride-price is still a common practice. Although the custom is declining, some wealthy Fon men take more than one wife.

In the rural coastal areas Fon families live in wooden stilt houses constructed of bamboo with palm thatched roofs. In inland

Fon carved altar slab from Benin.

areas the Fon reside in family compounds of mud houses arranged in a rectangular pattern. Most compounds include an open courtyard that serves as a gathering spot and a shrine that contains religious symbols.

In the urban areas the Fon usually dress in Western-style clothing, but traditional costumes can still be seen. Because of the intense heat, men wear trousers or shorts and short-sleeve shirts. Women wear long saronglike dresses of colorful cotton with their shoulders left bare, and they wrap bright turbans or scarves around their heads. Fon chiefs carry decorative parasols that are used as ornaments in marriage and other ceremonies, and for protection from the harsh sun. An ancient beauty practice of the Fon that is still practiced is the marking of the body with scars that are then dyed various colors.

The typical diet of the Fon revolves around starchy vegetables. A porridge made of millet or corn is a staple of most meals. Yams, pounded into a breadlike texture, are used to create a popular dish known as *fufu*. When deep fried, the yams are served as a dish called *dun dun*. Okra is used to thicken stews; and plantains are fried, salted, and eaten like potato chips. Meat, fish, and poultry are added to millet and stew dishes, but only occasionally. Many of the Fon recipes call for a sprinkle of a hot chili pepper called *pili pili*. After eating this scorchingly hot ingredient, the Fon like to wash down their food with *sodabe* (a strong palm wine) or millet beer.

The Fon religion is animist, which means they believe that objects in nature—water, trees, rocks, etc.—have spirits. Most of the Fon gods are represented by animals. The Fon also practice *vodu,* a form of voodoo that involves priests who use herbal medicines, charms, amulets, and other objects thought to have magical powers. Portable altars are used to worship the spirits of ancestors.

In larger Benin cities such as Abomey or Porto Novo, Fon art can be found in restored palaces. Historic tapestries, paintings, carvings, and sculptures trace the history of the Fon kingdom. Large wooden sculptures, decorated with metal, represent Fon warriors. The oral literature of the Fon is substantial and includes poems, songs, proverbs, riddles, and folktales. Modern literature, written by French-educated Fon, includes popular novels about Dahomey and short stories. The peasant and agrarian Fon are known for their vibrant songs and dances that offer praise to the natural spirits with the hope of receiving a fruitful harvest in return.

Today, the Fon are the largest ethnic group in Benin, representing 50 percent of the total population and the majority of the rural farming population. Nicephore Soglo, a Fon, has served as the country's president since 1991.

HAUSA
('how suh)

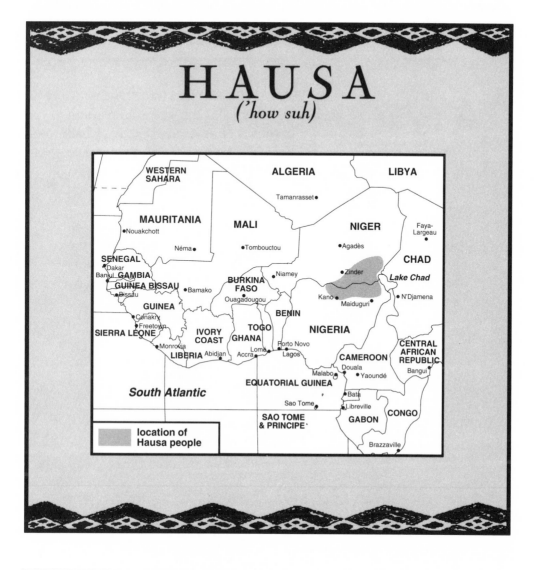

location of
Hausa people

POPULATION:	15,000,000
LOCATION:	Nigeria, Niger
LANGUAGE:	Hausa
PRIMARY FOODS:	Rice, sorghum, millet, peanuts

A RURAL WEST AFRICAN PEOPLE, THE HAUSA INHABIT THE PLA-
teau and plains areas of northern Nigeria and southeastern
Niger. Their territory is bordered on one side by Lake Chad
and extends almost to the Niger River on the other side. The
areas have an annual rainfall of 30–40 inches, with the wet season
extending from June through September, followed by a dry season
from October to May.

Folk stories tell of the existence of seven Hausa kingdoms, each
having a walled city called a *birni*. These walled cities dominated the
countryside that surrounded them, and by the 11th or 12th century
the territory-based system of the Hausa had resulted in the establish-
ment of commercial centers as well as agricultural production.

Because the territory of the Hausa was located in an area in
which trade routes, particularly for the trans-Saharan trade, had existed since prehistory, several developments in Hausa culture occurred. Most notable was the adoption of the Islamic religion at the
end of the 15th century. The Hausa were also exposed to the reli-

A Hausa man places stalks of millet into a granary in Chadawanka, Niger.

A Hausa woman pounds millet in front of her house in Chadawanka.

gious and worldly scholars who traveled the trade routes, and therefore developed a knowledge of writing and the law.

The trade routes also affected the economy and the population. Smaller chiefdoms evolved into larger kingdoms, and Hausa rulers called *Ha'be* became very powerful. With power came corruption and an increasing heavy-handedness toward their subjects through taxation and demands for labor.

The Hausa were predominantly an agricultural people who coexisted with the Fulani, who were nomadic herders. The Fulani also suffered under the Hausa rulers, and in the late 19th and early 20th centuries the two groups joined forces to revolt against the corruption of the elite Hausa. This revolt was known as a *jihad,* the Arab word for "holy war." Eventually, the revolt was successful, and the Hausa and Fulani were able to establish a loosely unified sultanate, in which the Fulani generally dominated. This sultanate survived

Young Hausa women from Chadawanka.

Hausa stucco relief designs from Niger/Nigeria.

until the British conquest of the area at the beginning of the 20th century.

The impact on the Hausa of European influences in the 19th and early 20th centuries was mainly economic and political. The slave trade was gradually abolished, and palm oil became the main export. The partitioning of West Africa by the European nations in the late 19th century led to the division of the Hausa homeland, isolating it from the rest of the region.

The Hausa were among the groups who sought and achieved independence for Nigeria in 1960, but it has always been difficult for the various government rulers to unify the many groups that

Pattern from Hausa embroidered cloth from Niger/Nigeria.

make up the country. The Hausa, Fulani, Yoruba, and Ibo all wanted a voice in the government. After decades of unrest and a series of coups, the Hausa settled into a relationship of relatively peaceful coexistence with their neighbors.

Today, the Hausa are the largest ethnic group in Nigeria, comprising over 20 percent of the total population. They live in small towns and large cities such as Sokoto and Kano, and farm the surrounding land, which is divided up into farms belonging to different households. They rarely travel far from their towns and receive their news from the outsiders who come from all over to trade on market day.

The basic unit of social organization is the *gida,* a household or compound. The gida is usually surrounded by a fence of earth and stalks with an open courtyard where the cooking area is located. Separate dwellings are built for the head of the household, his wife (or wives), and sometimes his married sons. There are also shelters for the animals and sometimes a shop for selling goods. Wealthier Hausa families build special passageways between the compounds to provide privacy for the women, who by Islamic law are not supposed to be seen in public.

Traditionally, a woman moves to her husband's gida after she marries him. Marriage among wealthier Hausa may occur when a girl is as young as 13 or 14, at which time she becomes a woman responsible for bearing and nurturing children, cooking meals, and making goods to sell in the compound shop or at the market. Barred by Islamic law from going to the market themselves, women often send their children to sell their products for them.

Hausa children are considered very important for the economic benefit they bring to the family and are treated well. Seven days after a Hausa child is born, the entire community joins in a special naming ceremony to welcome the child. Once the baby is named, its head is shaved and tattooed with markings that identify it as a Hausa member. As soon as they are old enough, Hausa boys help on the farms, planting and harvesting, and caring for the livestock. Some boys are sent to Western-style schools while others study the Koran, the Muslim holy book. Some girls receive an education, but most are expected to stay at home and help their mothers.

The main crops grown by the Hausa are sorghum and millet

for food, but other crops, such as rice, cotton, hemp, tobacco, peanuts, and henna, are grown for their commercial value. The Hausa practice crop rotation to allow the soil to regenerate and irrigate their fields with water from streams and wells.

No matter what they are doing, Hausa men and boys stop and pray together five times a day, as required by the Muslim faith. They celebrate two main religious festivals each year known as the "lesser" and "greater" festivals, each involving a month of fasting followed by a feast and gift giving. Those who can afford it make the religious pilgrimage to Mecca in Saudi Arabia at least once in their lives. In summary, the traditions of Islam are very strong among the Hausa, governing their outlook on life as well as their daily activities.

HUTU
(hoo too)

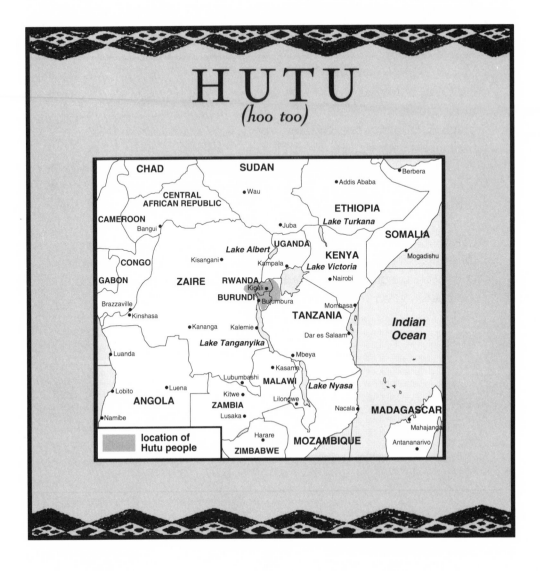

location of Hutu people

POPULATION:	5,000,000
LOCATION:	Rwanda, Burundi, Zaire, Tanzania
LANGUAGES:	Rwand, Rundi, Kirundi
PRIMARY FOODS:	Bananas, sorghum, peas, milk

A PEOPLE WHO HAVE ENDURED ETHNIC PREJUDICE AND REPRES-
sion for centuries, the Hutu live mostly in the rolling green
hills and lush valleys of Rwanda and Burundi in east central
Africa. The area contains several mountain ranges as well as many
rivers, lakes, and swamps. The climate is generally warm and humid
with rainfall averaging around 40–50 inches per year.

The early history of the Hutu is traced back to the 13th century
when several loosely structured kingdoms inhabited what is now
Rwanda and Burundi. Iron-using farmers, the Hutu had migrated
there from the surrounding regions in previous centuries and were
linked to other groups in the area who shared a similar belief in a
mythical figure known as Gihanga—the founder. Gihanga was an
ancestral king noted for his sacred drumming and fire ceremonies.

There is little recorded history of early Hutu life. What is
known, however, is that it changed dramatically during the 14th century when Tutsi cattle herders settled in Hutu territory. The Tutsi,
although much smaller in number than the Hutu, forced the Hutu
into a semislavery relationship known as "ubuhake." In the centuries that followed, the Hutu served as the backbone of the Tutsi
economy, tending cattle and providing agricultural goods and labor.
In exchange, the Hutu ware protected by the Tutsi from other competing peoples.

In essence, the Hutu became assimilated into Tutsi life, paying
taxes to the Tutsi king while turning over all profits to the Tutsi
people. The Hutu also adopted many Tutsi customs such as dances,
songs, and music and remained subservient for years.

In the late 1890s, the Germans colonized the Tutsi/Hutu territory, and about fifty years later the Belgians took over the area. The
Tutsi, a tall, thin, light-skinned people, were considered by the colo-
nialists to be more like the Europeans and superior to the Hutu who
were much shorter and darker in appearance. Because of this, the
colonizers favored the Tutsi by reserving places for them in government and granting them better access to education.

In the late 1950s and 1960s, the Hutu attempted several times
to rise up against the ruling Tutsi, and at one point killed thousands
of them. When independence came to Rwanda in the early 1960s,
the Hutu seized control of the government there. In Burundi, in

1972, the Hutu attempted to rise up against the Tutsi but were brutally defeated. So intent on retaining their power, the Tutsi in Burundi set about on a violent rampage against the Hutu, intentionally killing those who had higher levels of education, good jobs, and money. Thousands of Hutu homes were destroyed, and over 100,000 Hutus were killed.

Although many Hutu hold positions of power in both Burundi and Rwanda, violent ethnic clashes have been the norm for decades. In 1993, the leaders of both countries were killed when a plane in which they were flying was shot down by rebels. The tragic event sparked months of massive bloodshed for both the Hutu and the Tutsi. It is estimated that hundreds of thousands of Hutus have been killed since 1993, and thousands more have fled to nearby Tanzania and Zaire for refuge.

In both Rwanda and Burundi, the Hutu make up about 80 percent of the total population. Although many live in modern apartments in cities such as Kigali and Bujumbura, most Hutu maintain an agricultural lifestyle in rural villages where they live in family compounds known as "rugos." Within these compounds are several generations of one family surrounded by plots for farming. Most Hutus practice Christianity, which they adopted from the European colonists, but some ancient African customs prevail. A staple of the Hutu diet is bananas with a typical meal being a casserole of peas and bananas simmered in palm oil.

Unfortunately, due to the recent violence, hundreds of thousands of Hutu now live in makeshift camps where the sanitary conditions are deplorable and food and clean water are scarce.

IBO
(ee boh)

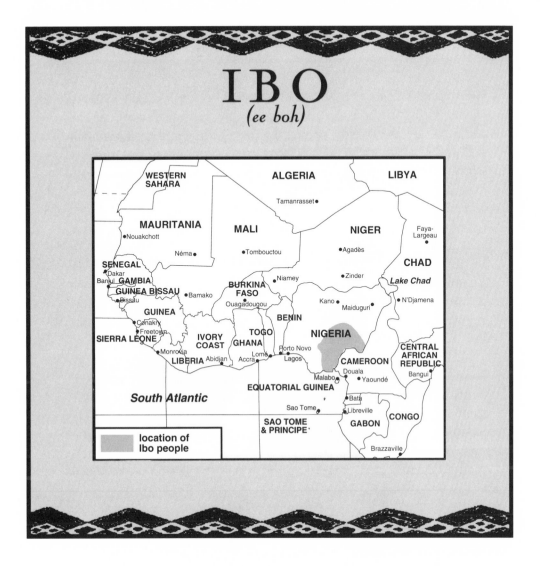

location of
Ibo people

POPULATION:	8,000,000
LOCATION:	Southeastern Nigeria
LANGUAGES:	Igbo, English
PRIMARY FOODS:	Yams, cassava, corn, beans, okra, fruits

IBOLAND LIES BETWEEN TWO RIVERS, THE NIGER TO THE WEST AND the Cross to the east. The areas along the rivers, as well as the delta, are thick with forests. To the north, the forests thin out and grassland predominates. The tropical climate has wet and dry seasons; the wet season lasts from February to August and again from September to November. The southern parts of Iboland receive as much as 100 inches of rain per year.

The ancestors of today's Ibo inhabited Iboland at least as far back as 5,000 years ago. Pottery shards dating from 4,500 years ago are remarkably similar to the pottery made by the Ibo today. Other archaeological evidence indicates that the Ibo were cultivating yams before 1000 B.C. and working iron before 500 B.C. Skill at ironworking was very instrumental in their development, because iron tools and weapons allowed great advances in agriculture and hunting.

Skilled ironwork also benefited the Ibo in the area of trade: Their finely crafted swords, hoes, axes, razors, bolts, and hinges were sought after by their neighbors. Both trading and agricultural development contributed to the flourishing of this culture. As the Ibo's economic skills evolved, so did their political organization. Unlike many other African societies, especially agricultural ones, they developed a decentralized organization in which the basic unit of social

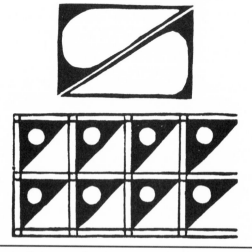

Ibo painted wall motifs from Nigeria.

Design molded on an Ibo clay pot from Nigeria.

life was the village, and within the village decisions were made col-
lectively. The individual Ibo enjoyed a remarkable amount of free-
dom in this comparatively democratic system.

In the early 16th century, European slave traders arrived and
changed Ibo society. For the next 300 years, first Portuguese, then
Dutch, and then English slave traders were more interested in
human beings than in either iron tools or agricultural products.
Many Ibo merchants became slave traders, securing their human
goods from the neighboring Yoruba in the interior. When that was

Wooden mask of an Ibo water spirit, from Nigeria.

Ibo carved funerary stone from Nigeria.

not convenient, they sold fellow Ibo to the Europeans. It is estimated that during the 18th and 19th centuries alone, more than
400,000 Ibo were taken from the coasts of eastern Nigeria.

Even after the European slave trade declined in the middle
1800s, it continued among the Ibo. Once the slave trade died down,
Europeans became more interested in palm oil, which was used as a
lubricant for industrial machinery. Ibo palm oil merchants used
slaves both to produce and to transport the oil.

Africa was rich in natural resources, and the European nations
set about colonizing the continent by the late 1800s. Great Britain
attempted to colonize Nigeria and encountered resistance among
the Ibo. Iboland was not thoroughly subdued until after World War
I; but even then the Ibo were not about to give in to foreign rule.
After coal was discovered in Iboland, the British made a greater
effort to bring it under control. Instead of working with the existing
system of local village control, the British imposed their own, auto-
cratic system, appointing local governors to govern the villages and
control the coal. The governors proved to be easily corrupted. The
Ibo women, who used the coal for cooking, began to protest against
the corrupt governors. The Women's War of 1929, which began as
a protest against the local governors, soon turned into a protest
against British colonial rule. While the British put down the protests

with firepower, and the women suffered many casualties, their protests taught the British not to take the tradition of Ibo self-government lightly.

The Ibo continued to fight against colonial rule until 1960, when Nigeria gained independence from Great Britain. After that, differences among the three main ethnic groups in Nigeria—Ibo, Yoruba, and Hausa—led to government coups and designated regions for each group. Although the government took no action to transport the groups to these areas, attacks on Ibos living in the north in 1966 caused over one million of them to move to their designated eastern region.

In 1967, the Ibo military governor declared this eastern region independent of Nigeria and formed the Republic of Biafra. Nigeria considered this move to be an outright rebellion and attacked. In the 30-month war that followed, over a million Nigerians, most of them Ibos, died, many from starvation and disease. In spite of bitterness on both sides, Ibo and the other main ethnic groups in Nigeria were able to come to terms, and Ibos have been largely successful in reintegrating into Nigerian society.

Ibo social and cultural practices vary widely and have been strongly influenced in some areas by contact with the Yoruba and the British. Villages are often carefully planned, with broad streets and buildings made of clay and painted bright patterns of red, yellow, and black. Roofs are made of thatch or tin. Traditionally, men and women occupied separate houses, but now an entire family is more likely to inhabit one house.

Ibo men grow the yams that are the basis of the Ibo diet; women raise other vegetables. Women also transport water and firewood, sell the excess produce at markets, and do the cooking. A typical Ibo meal consists of boiled mashed yams called *fufu* along with beans and other vegetables, palm oil and bits of meat or fish, and fresh bananas, oranges, and pineapples.

The Ibo are among the most literate peoples of Africa, largely because of a strong tradition of attending Christian missionary schools after the British conquest of Iboland in the early 1900s. Many Ibo have adopted Christianity, but they also continue to practice some of the older religious traditions, such as ancestor worship and the belief in herbal cures.

The Ibo have maintained many of the artistic talents of their ancestors, including music, dance, painting, and sculpture, and many decorate their homes with traditional hand-crafted clay and wood statues. They have also placed a great deal of emphasis on formal education and can claim a substantial body of literature in both English and their native Igbo language. Well-known Ibo writers include Pita Nwana, author of *Omenuko,* and Chinua Achebe, author of *A Man of the People* and *Things Fall Apart.*

KAMBA
(kahm ba)

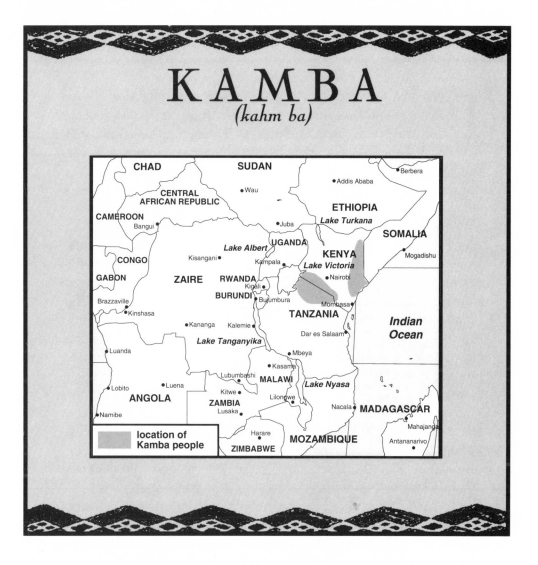

location of Kamba people

POPULATION: 1,500,000
LOCATION: Kenya and northern Tanzania
LANGUAGES: Kiswahili, Kikamba, English
PRIMARY FOODS: Grains, pumpkin, potatoes, bananas, beans, meat

PRIMARILY FARMERS AND TRADERS, THE KAMBA LIVE IN EASTERN Kenya, southwestern Kenya not far from the Indian Ocean, and the northern boundaries of Tanzania. The land varies from arid, hilly steppe regions to the highlands of majestic Mt. Kilimanjaro. Much of this area, which is known as Kambaland, is burdened by frequent bouts of drought that render the area's streams dirt dry for months at a time.

The history of the Kamba can be traced back to the 1500s when they lived in the Kilimanjaro plains and survived by raising cattle. In the early 1700s, the Kamba were challenged by members of the neighboring Maasai who wanted control of their land in order to support their own cattle. Rather than battle with the Maasai, the Kamba emigrated northeastward. During the following 200 years, they continued to spread out amid the higher, hilly areas and the steppe regions to the east. Many of them became skilled farmers utilizing elaborate irrigation systems and terraced fields for their crops.

From the late 1700s to the middle 1800s, many of the Kamba made their living as merchants, trading in slaves, ivory, medicines, and food. Kamba caravans monopolized much of the trade route that crossed from the desert areas to the eastern coast. But later on, Swahili clans seized control of most of the trade routes, and the Kamba then concentrated their merchant skills on the sale of ivory. In the late 1800s, the British took control of the area. Because the Kamba had no formal chiefs or central government, Kambaland was easily divided into small districts by the British. During the First and Second World Wars, many Kamba men served in the British army.

After a series of anticolonial rebellions during the 1950s, independence from the British was achieved in Kenya in 1963. Following independence, the new government tried to persuade the Kamba to relinquish their clan loyalties in favor of loyalty to the Kenyan government, and many of them did. As the fourth largest ethnic group in the country, the Kamba played an increasingly important role in the Kenyan government throughout the 1960s and 1970s. Today, the Kamba are very much a part of the government and work hard at ensuring that Kamba traditions are not ignored by modern society.

Many of the Kamba now reside in cities—such as Nairobi and

Kamba carvers at work in Mombasa, Kenya.

Mombasa in Kenya, and Arusha in Tanzania—where they live in concrete-block apartment houses. A large number still dwell in small villages, or *gates,* which support a group of related families. A gate usually consists of 12 or more houses. Several of these gates form a clan, which can contain as many as 50,000 people. Each clan can be identified by its own symbol, known as a *totem.*

Only about four feet high, traditional Kamba houses are constructed of branches and mud and have a sloping thatched roof. More modern houses are made of brick with roofs of iron. Inside there are two fireplaces: a central one used for cooking, and a smaller one for heating the sleeping areas. A cattle shed and grain storage bin are usually adjacent to the houses. These small, squat houses serve as shelter for large, extended families. Typically, a husband and one or more wives, their children, and relatives live together. Sometimes, husbands keep separate houses on their homesteads for additional wives and children.

As in many other African cultures, the Kamba social structure revolves around age-sets. During their teenage years, Kamba boys

The finished carvings on display.

and girls are divided into separate groups and given a teacher who offers instruction on duties such as hunting, cattle raising, and cooking. Male age-sets include boy, young man/warrior, middle-aged man, and old man. Female age-sets include girl, single woman, married woman, old woman, and childless woman. Transitions from one age-set to the next are marked with elaborate rituals.

Trading, hunting, farming, and herding all produce revenue for the Kamba economy. Using bows and arrows, Kamba men hunt for animals that can provide valuable hides used for clothing and trade. They also cultivate tobacco, coffee, and cotton as cash crops. For their own diet, they grow maize, millet, peas, beans, cassava, pumpkins, and potatoes. Typical Kamba meals include stewed or roasted

Kamba patterns for wooden stools with hammered
wire decorations, from Kenya.

green bananas, porridge sweetened with honey, and grain dishes
complemented with slivers of meat. In recent years, soil depletion
and droughts have made farming difficult for the Kamba, and many
have accepted employment with the government and abandoned
their farming traditions.

In small villages, many of the Kamba still wear clothing made
of handwoven cloth or animal hides. The women wrap the material
around their bodies and tie it at one shoulder. Some wear leather
aprons adorned with brass studs or an ornamental corset made of
beads. Traditional male dress consists of a long hide or cloth skirt
that reaches below the knees and a blanket draped over their shoul-

ders. Kamba who live in cities wear European-style dresses, shirts, and pants. Traditional Kamba jewelry is made of copper wires that are molded into rings, necklaces, and bracelets. Some of the Kamba file a triangular space between their two upper middle teeth as a form of body decoration.

Although the influence of British missionaries meant that many of the Kamba converted to Christianity, aspects of their native religion remain an important part of their life. Traditional religious customs include belief in one central God, the presence of ancestor spirits, and an afterlife where the dead are reunited with loved ones and friends. In religious ceremonies, songs and dances are performed to ward off *aimu* (ancient ancestors who return as evil spirits). The Kamba also believe that some people possess powers that enable them to cause harm to others. To protect against this harm, they enlist the help of healers, who happen to be both male and female, and utilize charms and potions to generate good luck.

Known for their creativity, the Kamba put great emphasis on the arts and incorporate music, dance, storytelling, and games into their day-to-day lives. They sing songs while working at home and in the fields; and use drums, bells, rattles, and gourds to create background music. They entertain themselves with proverbs, word games, riddles, and poems that have been passed down through the generations. And their talent as skilled wood-carvers has earned them respect and appreciation for their art throughout the world.

KHOISAN

(ʼkoy sahn)

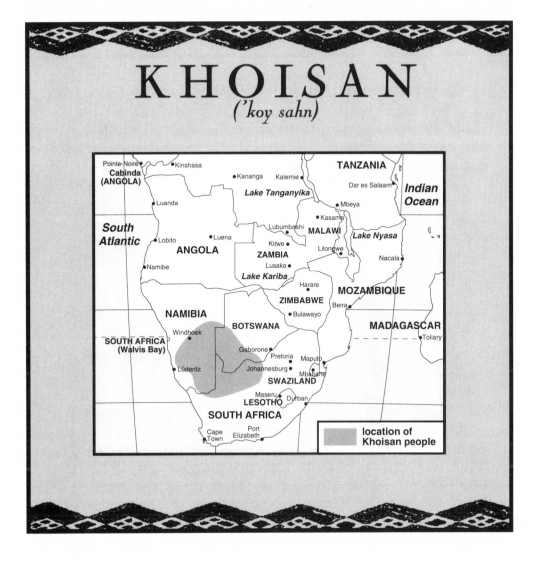

POPULATION:	55,000
LOCATION:	Botswana, Namibia, South Africa
LANGUAGES:	The many dialects of the Khoisan language
PRIMARY FOODS:	Root vegetables, fruit, meat

DESCENDANTS OF AN ANCIENT PEOPLE LIVING BEFORE 500 B.C. who once inhabited a long stretch of land that ran from Ethiopia southward to the Cape of Good Hope, the Khoisan now live at the southwestern tip of Africa. Their territory is a varied landscape of green coastlines and dry, flat steppe regions.

The history of the Khoisan in the region where they are today dates back to the 14th century when they migrated southward from Ethiopia and settled on land that was suitable to their hunting-and-gathering tradition. Two distinct groups developed: One resided in the Kalahari Desert, and the other lived along the coast and called itself Khoikhoi Khoisan. During the 1400s, the Khoisan began trading with the Portuguese. By the mid-1600s, the Dutch, English, and French set up trading posts in Khoisan territory, and both the groups began to lose their land and independence.

Today, most of the Khoisan have intermarried with other native cultures, such as the Bantus, or with descendants of the European settlers. Owing to population expansion and development throughout southern Africa, less than one-third of the Khoisan remain independent herders and farmers. These few traditionalists live in temporary huts made of woven grass and still wear loincloths and aprons as their basic clothing. The men hunt for antelope using arrows dipped in poison made from snake venom and poisonous plants. The women pick fruits and vegetables and collect water with dried ostrich eggshells. Some common meals for the Khoisan include pumpkin stew with bits of lamb, boiled cassava, ground beef simmered with curry and ginger, and cornmeal porridge.

The Khoisan who reside closer to urban developments live in small, permanent houses and work on large commercial farms, or on fishing fleets along the coast. For the most part, the urban Khoisan have adopted Western-styles of dress and buy their food from modern grocery stores.

For one month each year, large groups of several Khoisan families gather for an annual get-together that serves as a form of recreation as well as a means of passing on the oral histories of their past. Since marriages within families are taboo, this gathering is also a time for parents to arrange marriages for their children.

Although the Khoisan have no written language, they do have

a long history of folktales, stories, and fables. Listening to these stories is especially enjoyable because the Khoisan language is accented
with unusual clicking sounds. They also have a unique type of music
that is played on various instruments, including the mouth organ, a
thumb piano, and a guitarlike instrument called a *gwashi*.

KIKUYU
(kee 'koo yoo)

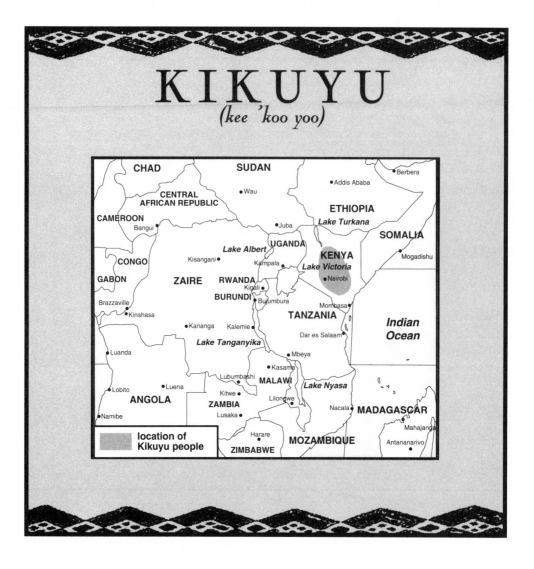

POPULATION:	3,000,000
LOCATION:	Kenya
LANGUAGES:	Kikuyu (a Bantu dialect), English
PRIMARY FOODS:	Milk, maize, sweet potatoes, bananas, manioc, beans, chicken, goat

THE MOST INFLUENTIAL GROUP OF PEOPLE WITHIN THE COUNTRY of Kenya, the Kikuyu live in the Great Rift Valley of Kenya, which runs through the center of the country from Lake Rudolf in the north to Lake Victoria in the south. Much of the area possesses a dramatic landscape marked by the 17,000-foot Mt. Kenya, rushing streams, heavy rains, and rich soil made fertile from volcanic ash.

According to ancient folklore, the founder of the Kikuyu was a man named Gikuyu who was taken to a summit by a divine spirit and commanded to establish a homestead near a cluster of fig trees. Gikuyu's wife, Muumbi, had nine daughters, and each of these daughters now represents one of the nine Kikuyu clans that bear their names. The nine clans of the Kikuyu are: Achera, Agachiku, Airimu, Aithaga, Aitherandu, Ambui, Angare, Angui, and Anjiru. Modern history notes that during the 1500s the Kikuyu began acquiring land and spreading throughout what is now the Kikuyu territory. As the groups grew larger, they created *mbaris,* or related clans, and began forming organized communities that traded with other cultures in the area.

Although the Kikuyu were threatened by the Maasai during the 1700s, and struck with a smallpox epidemic during the 1800s, they managed to maintain a stronghold on their land. In the 1890s, the British seized control of Kenya and began confiscating Kikuyu properties. Unable to defend themselves against the military power of the British, the Kikuyu yielded much of their land. But they were not so willing to merge culturally with the British, and during the 1920s they formed their own independent school system. This system places great emphasis on formal education and is one of the reasons why there are so many Kikuyu teachers, lawyers, and doctors in Kenya today.

Following World War II, dissatisfaction with the British government grew among the beleaguered Kikuyu. In an effort to regain their independence, they banded together as armed groups known as *Mau Mau.* Beginning in 1952 they set in motion a rebellion that would be remembered years later as one of the most brutal uprisings against colonialism in African history. When it ended in 1956, over 3,000 Kikuyu were killed. But the uprising prompted the British to surrender Kenya to self-rule and eventually to grant its indepen-

Kikuyu men who have coated their bodies with a mixture of animal fat and clay.

dence (in 1963). The new government, led by Kikuyu President
Jomo Kenyatta, set forth a policy of land reform that returned much
of the confiscated Kikuyu land to its original owners.

Today the Kikuyu coalition, known as the Kenya African
Union, is the most powerful political party in Kenya, and the Kikuyu
comprise 16 percent of the country's population. The Kikuyu are
one of the largest, most educated, and socially active groups in
Kenya. Some of this influence, however, has led to internal strife
between the poorer Kikuyu and the wealthy Kikuyu business leaders. This strife was evident in 1975, when a Kikuyu leader who op-
posed the ruling Kikuyu elite was assassinated.

Kikuyu who don't live in large cities continue to base their social structure around smaller homesteads. Typically, a homestead is
situated along a ridge with a large stream nearby. The extended family mbari that lives in this homestead can contain anywhere from
50 to 1,000 people. Kikuyu mbaris are well-organized, totally self-

An elderly Kikuyu man trims his beard in this photograph from Kenya taken in the early 1900s.

Engraving from a wooden Kikuyu dancing board,
from Kenya.

sufficient economic units. Occasionally, people who are not related
to the family are allowed to rent space in the mbari.

A typical Kikuyu house is either round or rectangular, with mud
walls and a thatched or tin roof. As a polygamous culture, husbands
often have more than one wife. In this case, each wife and her children have their own dwelling and are responsible for contributing to
the overall economy of the family. Boys are sometimes separated
from their immediate families and are housed in special bachelor
houses. Following a patrilineal tradition, a male and his family remain with his father's extended family. When a woman marries, she
becomes a member of her husband's mbari.

Most of the Kikuyu today continue to support themselves
through agriculture. But because of dramatic increases in population, land ownership for farming remains a heated issue. Whether
they have small family plots or large, commercial farms, all Kikuyu
are very territorial about the land they own. With an abundance of
fertile soil, they cultivate coffee, tea, and bananas as cash crops;
and maize, bananas, sweet potatoes, rice, and beans for their own
consumption. Cattle are raised for milk and milk products rather

than for meat. Chickens and goats are raised for consumption but only as a supplement to the Kikuyu's primarily vegetarian diet.

Age-sets, with stages from birth through old age, remain the primary social hierarchy of Kikuyu life. Six stages of life are recognized, each with its own duties and responsibilities. Regardless of what mbari they belong to, all male members of a particular age-set are initiated into that age-set the same year and consider themselves brothers throughout their lives. Usually, a group of male age-set members rule over their mbari for about 30 years and then pass their power on to the next generation in a formal ceremony.

While many of the Kikuyu converted to Christianity during the period of British control, most tried to incorporate their older customs into their newly adopted religion. Today, most of the Kikuyu worship a single god known as Ngai and still believe in the powerful influence of ancestor spirits. Sheep and goats are occasionally used for religious sacrifice.

The traditional style of dress of the Kikuyu has for the most part been abandoned. Years ago they wore clothing made of goatskin and decorated their bodies with metal jewelry; ornate headdresses made of feathers, leather, and beads; and hairstyles adorned with mud and string. Today, most Kikuyu wear Western-style dresses, skirts, shirts, and pants. On special holidays, however, traditional costumes are worn for celebrations. Kikuyu crafts include pots for cooking, woven baskets made from sisal or bark, arrowheads, spears, swords, cowbells, and rattles.

KONGO

('kon go)

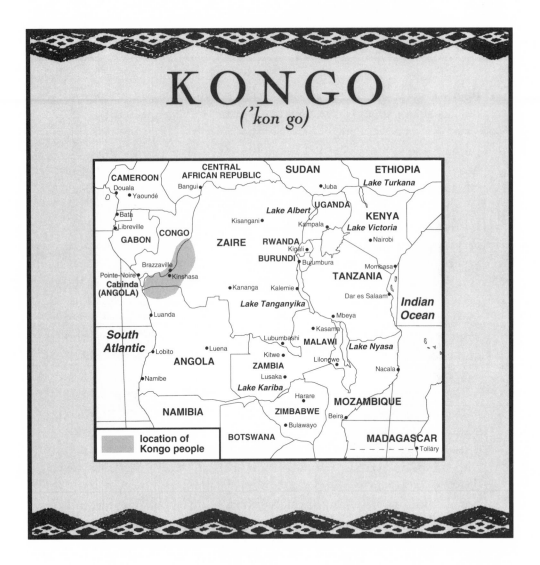

location of Kongo people

POPULATION:	6,000,000
LOCATION:	Angola, Zaire, and Congo
LANGUAGES:	Kikongo, French
PRIMARY FOODS:	Maize, manioc, rice, peanuts, bananas

CALLED BaKongo BY THE PEOPLE THEMSELVES, THE Kongo have a past that is steeped in the grim reality of the slave trade. They live in central West Africa in the area that surrounds the Zaire River. Formerly called the Congo River, the Zaire is the seventh longest river on earth and snakes its way along a 2,600-mile arc from the heart of the continent eastward toward the Atlantic Ocean. A spectacular waterway full of whirlpools, rough waves, gorges, and ravines, the Zaire serves as the spine of the Kongo's homeland.

Southwestern Congo, western Zaire (formerly called Congo), and northwestern Angola make up the land of the Kongo people. The northern sections of the area have pockets of rain forests; the southern parts are predominantly savannas. Along the coastal areas the land is marked with thick woods and grasslands. Some of the river's valleys are punctuated with rolling hills and rugged mountains.

The history of the Kongo dates back to the last millennium B.C. in the lower Zaire River region where their ancestors, Bantu farmers, inhabited the forests and woodland areas. In the 1300s, several Kongo kingdoms existed along the banks of the river. By the 1400s, the kingdom of Kongo, in what today is Angola, absorbed several other cultures and became one of the most powerful kingdoms in Africa. Throughout that century, Kongo chiefs controlled much of the trade routes that crisscrossed from the interior to the coast. The Kongo king was a powerful man who owned numerous slaves and a harem of wives. He supervised a vast network of Kongo officials who collected taxes from the villages, and controlled the supply of goods that passed through the kingdom.

During the late 1400s, Portuguese explorers encountered the Kongo people and engaged in trade with the king. In 1491, under the influence of Portuguese missionaries, the Kongo king converted to Christianity, as did many of his people. For the next 200 years, Kongo kings aligned with the Portuguese in order to maintain control of their kingdom and found that the slave trade was a lucrative business that could make them even richer. Along with selling Africans from other kingdoms, the Kongo kings captured and sold members of their own people. To gain more control of the slave trade, the Portuguese launched a war against the Kongo in the mid-

Kongo weekly market near Mbanza-Nguneu, Zaire.

1600s, brutally defeating the Kongo army in 1665. In the northern regions, the French took control of the coffee and cocoa plantations. During the next 200 years, the Kongo kingdom was divided into several small chiefdoms, and the king lost power to local chiefs, who continued to take part in the slave trade.

By the mid-1800s, the slave trade was outlawed by European countries, and the Kongo chiefs lost their substantial income. In 1885, Belgium gained control of the Kongo region and renamed it the Belgian Congo. After an epidemic of sleeping sickness that killed many of the Kongo people in the early 1900s, the Kongo regained their strength. They achieved independence in 1964 and became the Republic of Zaire in 1971. Angola gained its independence in 1974.

In recent years, many Kongo have moved to large cities, such as Kinshasa in Zaire and Brazzaville in Congo, and have adopted a modern way of life. But most still live in traditional Kongo villages, which are organized around clans. The typical village houses about 75 families from the same clan. Rectangular houses, built of brick

Pattern on a carved Kongo sculpture from
Brazzaville, Zaire.

with straw, palm thatch, or corrugated tin roofs, are laid out in a gridlike pattern. In the past, houses were simpler, consisting of wood poles and palm branch roofs.

Kongo family life is based on the sharing of responsibilities. Women's primary duties are working the fields and preparing the family's food. Men are responsible for building and maintaining houses, hunting, fishing, and producing plant products such as palm wine. Kongo tradition encourages trial marriages so that couples can see if they are compatible. A groom's family offers a payment to the bride before marriage. Boys and girls are usually separated at the age of six and are taught their duties by their same-sex parent.

Although they occasionally eat small portions of meat and fish, the Kongo are mainly vegetarians. Staples of their diet include maize, manioc, bananas, peanuts, rice, eggplant, tomatoes, beans, peppers, fruits, and nuts. Fiery hot peppers are used to add flavor to their meals. Palm wine, made from palm trees, is a Kongo specialty.

Kongo are well-known for their fabrics, and Kongo cloth was a prized export when the region was a kingdom. Made of palm fibers and produced on a loom, Kongo cloth is as smooth as silk. Weaving also provides the Kongo with mats for bedding and decoration. The traditional style of dress for women is a long cloth wrapped around the waist, with another piece wrapped around the torso. Most Kongo men have given up their loose, caftanlike clothing and adopted the European pants-and-shirts style of dress.

Tropical illnesses such as malaria, sleeping sickness, tuberculosis, and intestinal parasites have plagued the Kongo for centuries. Although in recent years modern health organizations have helped control the diseases, many Kongo still rely on remedies like herbs, charms, and blessings from a natural healer.

Many of the Kongo people converted to Christianity during

Kongo soapstone carving from Angola.

colonial rule, but the religion never fully took hold and customs of their original religion are still practiced. Traditional reverence for ancestors remains a focal point, and rainmaking ceremonies, puberty rites, and the use of sacred amulets to bring good luck are still common. Many Kongo homes contain ancestor shrines where families pray for the dead.

Religious beliefs are also tied to the arts and crafts of the Kongo. Artisans and blacksmiths have high status, equal to that of priests and chiefs. Those who produce iron weapons for hunting are thought to possess the ability to ward off evil. Along with their lead and copper jewelry that is worn by both men and women to designate social status, the Kongo are well-known for their wood carvings and stone sculptures. Small statues, called guardians, are very popular. The fertility statue, usually representing a mother and child, is a common decoration in Kongo households. Some Kongo artwork combines Christian and African symbols, demonstrating how the Kongo have adjusted to the modern world while still honoring their culture's heritage.

KRU
(crew)

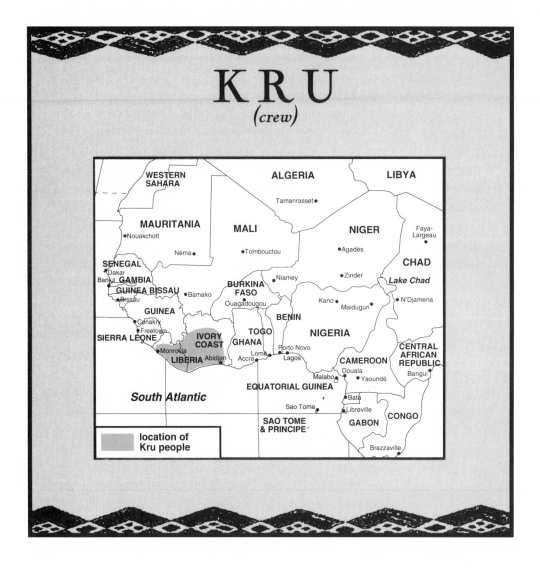

location of
Kru people

POPULATION: 85,000
LOCATION: Liberia, the Ivory Coast
LANGUAGES: Kru, English
PRIMARY FOODS: Fish, crab, rice, cassava, plantains, vegetables

SKILLFUL SAILORS, SHIPBUILDERS, AND FISHERMEN, THE KRU LIVE on the west coast of Africa in the countries of Liberia and the Ivory Coast. This low coastal region is marked by a series of lagoons, marshes, inlets, and natural harbors; and six major rivers that empty into the Atlantic Ocean. Dozens of sandy beaches dotted with palm trees line the coast. North of the coastline, the land rises to an altitude of 2,000 feet and is covered with dense tropical vegetation.

The history of the Kru dates back to the 16th century when they migrated from various parts of West Africa and settled along the coastline where they quickly established themselves as fishermen and sailors. During the 18th century, European colonizers were active in the slave trade along the coast, and many Kru went to work as seamen on their ships. When the British tried to capture some of the Kru in order to turn them into slaves, they resisted and worked out a compromise that would make both the Kru and the British happy. The Kru allowed the British to transport the slaves through their territory, but only if they left the Kru alone. To avoid any confusion, the Kru branded themselves with a thin line tattoo down the center of their foreheads so that the British would recognize them as Kru. With time, the Kru began capturing members of neighboring ethnic groups and trading them to the British. They also worked as sailors aboard the slave ships that transported slaves to Europe.

The Kru were such competent maritime workers that the British promoted them to positions as cooks, stevedores, and interpreters aboard their ships. When the slave trade was banned in the 19th century, the Kru continued to work on the European ships, loading cargo such as vegetables and ivory, and piloting the ships through the coastal harbors.

During the early 1800s, the American National Colonization Society had helped 6,000 freed African-American slaves move to Africa and settle in what is now Liberia. In 1847 the country gained its independence, and many of these African-Americans became government officials. The Kru, who resented the Americans' presence and felt that they had too much power within the government, staged an uprising in 1915. The government attempted to hold on to its power by destroying several Kru villages. During the 1930s, the Kru once again revolted. This time around, many of them aban-

Kru entertainers in Monrovia, Liberia.

doned their traditional villages and settled elsewhere; many moved to the Ivory Coast. Finally, in 1944, the government of Liberia granted better representation to the Kru and other indigenous peoples.

Although their total population is relatively small today, the Kru are divided into more than a dozen subgroups, each with its own dialect and variation in lifestyle. The Kru also have many villages throughout the coasts of both Liberia and the Ivory Coast. Most of these villages are located near one of the six rivers that cross through the region. In each Kru village a chief is in charge, but the community also abides by the rules of the national government.

Traditional Kru houses are rectangular, with mud walls and thatched or corrugated iron roofs. In the larger cities like Monrovia, the Kru live in modern concrete block houses.

These days, the Kru continue to turn to the ocean as a source for their livelihood. Many work as laborers in the shipping and fishing industries, and as shipbuilders and boat captains. Others build their own canoe-shaped boats and fish the waters using nets, lines, and traps. Young Kru boys learn these skills from their fathers at an early age. Kru women raise rice, peanuts, cassava, and vegetables to supplement their seafood-based diet. Along with raising crops, many Kru women now work outside the home as teachers, nurses, and civil servants. Children in the Kru culture are considered to be a sign of wealth, and a childless couple, no matter how much material wealth they may acquire, are considered to be poor.

Having had a great deal of contact with Europeans throughout the past 200 years, the Kru have abandoned traditional clothes and adopted a modern, Western-style of dress. Men wear shorts or pants and short-sleeve shirts; women and young girls wear bright colored cotton dresses and often wrap a matching cloth around their heads as a turban.

Typical meals of the Kru include spicy seafood gumbos with tomatoes and okra, grain dishes with bits of fish, a sweet bread made from bananas, crab soups, and sardines. Fish is also dried and salt-cured to be eaten when no fresh catch is available.

Most of the Kru consider themselves Christians, and a small number are Muslims. But their native religious customs are still present in their lives and are very much a part of their identity. Like many other native African cultures, the Kru believe in one supreme god, spirits that exist in nature, and the spirits of their ancestors. In their traditional religious ceremonies, they ask the ancestor spirits to protect the men when they go out to sea and bless them with a good bounty of fish. The Kru also have a long history of oral traditions, including proverbs, riddles, and folktales that praise their maritime heritage.

MAASAI
('mah sigh)

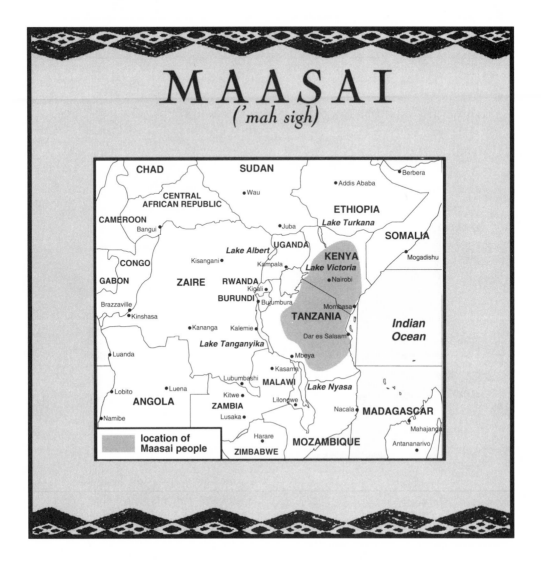

POPULATION:	100,000
LOCATION:	Kenya and Tanzania
LANGUAGE:	Maasai
PRIMARY FOODS:	Milk, cheese, meat, animal blood

THE MAASAI HAVE BEEN KNOWN THROUGHOUT AFRICA AS WAR-riors who possess great strength and a strong sense of inde-pendence. They live in the countries of Kenya and Tanzania, in an area known as Maasailand, which is home to some of the world's great natural wonders, including Mt. Kilimanjaro and the Ngorongoro Crater. Topographically, this part of East Africa varies from dense rain forests to broad savannas to grassy highland plains. In the highlands, the soil is fertile and some of the Maasai cultivate crops. In the lower savanna regions, the land is too dry for growing crops, but the grass is ideally suited for raising cattle.

The history of the Maasai dates back to an ancient people who lived along the Nile River in southern Sudan around 500 B.C. More recent ancestors lived in northern Kenya and included people who migrated from the southern regions of Ethiopia. With time, the Maasai migrated southward into the area that is now Tanzania. Throughout the mid-1800s, the Maasai were one of the most power-ful peoples in Africa, ruling over 10 million acres of land. During the early 1900s, British colonizers controlled parts of East Africa. In an effort to gain more control of the continent, they tried to recruit Maasai men into military service and also attempted to persuade them to enroll their children in British schools. The Maasai resisted and tried not to allow outside influences to alter their preferred way of life.

Within the Maasai, there are several different clans. Most of the clans are pastoral people and remain in permanent homesteads where they live entirely off the products of domestic animals. Some of the clans are more agricultural and cultivate crops in addition to animals. Depending upon the climate where they live, some of the clans move from place to place with the seasons.

The typical shelter is a small building made from branches and cattle manure that has been baked in the sun. The men build the framework, and the women fill in the walls. Each structure houses one family and contains beds, benches, and a hearth for cooking. A typical Maasai village, known as a *boma,* is based on kinship and contains several families. Within each village, rectangular houses are arranged in a circle and surrounded by a thorn fence. Livestock are kept in a pen in the center of the circle during the night and taken out for grazing during the day.

Maasai men selling hides to an Arab dealer in what is now Ntira, Tanzania, 1947.

Pmuni, a 13-year-old Maasai girl from Olengaitoli, Kenya, in 1959.

Since the Maasai are a polygamous culture, men tend to have more than one wife. Each wife lives with her children, and the husband divides his time between each of his families. Women often join together and share the responsibilities of domestic work and child care. Maasai elders and young warriors live as groups in their own houses.

An important aspect of Maasai life is the age-set system. Each adult male belongs to an age-set, a group which has specific duties, privileges, and authority throughout the clan. At the age of 16, a boy is circumcised and enters into his first age-set, the warrior. Warriors are responsible for protecting the village and its animals. Boys remain warriors for between 7 and 14 years and then achieve elder status. From then on, they move up the age-set scale into various levels of elderhood. Senior elders command great respect and are responsible for making important decisions.

Most of the Maasai keep goats and sheep, but cattle are their most prized livestock. So much so that cattle in the Maasai culture are treated with as much respect as family members. According to a Maasai folktale, God brought cattle to the earth specifically for ancient Maasai. This folktale is the foundation for their belief that all cattle on the earth should rightfully belong to them and once justified their reputation for violent cattle raids against other cultures.

By and large, the Maasai continue to live simply, relying almost entirely on their cattle for sustenance. From cattle they get milk, cheese, meat, and occasionally blood which is mixed with milk and used to supplement their diet. Beer made from honey is part of their diet but is reserved for special occasions.

Their cattle also provide them with dung for cooking fuel; hides for skirts, thongs, cloaks, and bedding; fat for baby food; and urine for cleansing. Even the cattle horns are turned into containers for storing food.

Maasai women customarily shave their heads. Maasai men wear their hair in neat rows of long, thin braids and apply cow grease and clay to keep it well groomed. Both men and women spend a great deal of time adorning their bodies with jewelry. The men wear earrings, headbands, and bead necklaces. The women adorn their necks and arms with colorful copper wires and beaded iron. To avoid irritation, they coat their skin with grease and leaves underneath the heavy jewelry. Warriors occasionally hold bundles of aromatic leaves under their armpits as a deodorant.

Celebrations and rituals play an important role in the life of the Maasai. Some of them are joyous and playful, like the naming ceremony for newborn babies, and the celebrations that honor men as they move from one age-set to the next. Others are painful, like circumcision in adolescent males and females, which marks their transition into adulthood and enables them to marry.

Storytelling, a tradition passed down through the generations, is a favorite activity among the Maasai. Entire villages gather around to listen as elders tell spellbinding stories of ancient warriors who fought off marauding leopards and killed them with their bare hands. Dancing and singing are also popular. Occasionally, Maasai dancers become so enthralled with their vigorous movements that they slip into a mystical, trancelike state. Maasai songs, usually sung by large groups, praise ancient warriors, cattle, and the beauty of women.

The Maasai do not believe in an afterlife, but they do believe in a god. They call their god Ngai, which is the same word used for sky. Maasai pray to this god for health, children, rain, and the safety of their cattle. When a Maasai dies, family members dress the body in new sandals and place a blade of grass in the hands as a peace offering. Instead of burying it, they leave the body in the grasslands to become food for wild animals.

Severe droughts in recent years have caused the death of many cattle and made life difficult for the Maasai. In an effort to help the Maasai, the governments of Kenya and Tanzania have encouraged them to become part of modern African society. Some of the Maasai have been forced by circumstance to move to cities and enroll their children in modern schools. But for the most part, the Maasai have chosen not to be assimilated into modern culture and remain loyal to their traditional way of life.

MALINKE

(mah 'leen key)

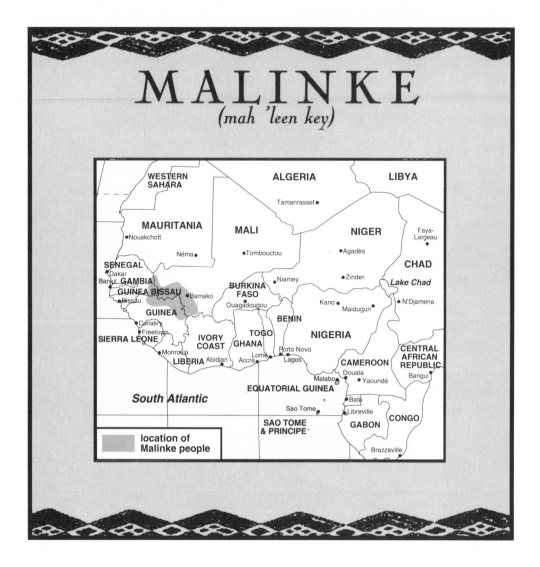

location of
Malinke people

POPULATION: 700,000
LOCATION: Senegal, Mali, and Guinea
LANGUAGES: Malinke (Mandingo), French
PRIMARY FOODS: Millet, rice, sorghum, milk, cheese, vegetables, beans, fish

MADE FAMOUS BY ALEX HALEY'S STORY OF THE KINTE FAMILY in his book *Roots,* the Malinke were once a powerful force in the kingdom of Mali. Also called Mandingo, the Malinke inhabit several countries in Africa but are most concentrated in the river regions of West Africa in Senegal, Mali, and Guinea. Most of the Malinke territory is dry, dotted with thorny bushes and low scrub forests. But along the riverbanks, lush tropical plants and wild animals are abundant, and heavy rains soak the land each summer.

Malinke history dates back to the 10th century, when they lived along the Niger River in the area that is now Mali. The land, rich with gold and iron deposits, enabled them to amass great wealth. During the 11th century, the Malinke *mansa* (king) converted to Islam and made the traditional Muslim pilgrimage to the holy city of Mecca. While on his long journey, the king established trade relations with other peoples that would serve the Malinke well for years to come. In following centuries, Malinke kings acquired more territory and wealth and secured lucrative trading agreements throughout West Africa that would make the Malinke one of the most powerful and richest empires on the continent.

Mansa Musa, one of the most revered Malinke kings, ruled during the 14th century and added even more wealth and prestige to his kingdom. Mansa Musa governed with absolute power and maintained a personal entourage that included dozens of slaves and a large group of poets called *jeli,* who recorded historic events and negotiated territorial disputes for the king. During his reign, massive Malinke caravans carrying tons of gold swept across the trade routes of northwestern Africa. Some traveled with over 40,000 people at one time.

Following Mansa Musa's death, the Malinke slowly slipped into decline and eventually separated into several self-governing kingdoms. In the early 1900s, the French gained control of much of West Africa, and the Malinke fell under the control of their power. But in 1960, Mali gained its independence, and many Malinke were incorporated into the new government. The same is true in the countries of Senegal and Guinea.

Today, many of the Malinke still live in independent territories under the rule of kings who are descendants of ancient royalty. Within the culture, there are several diverse groups, each linked his-

A 1915 photograph of a Malinke weaver.

torically by ancestral lineage. A class system, based on ancestral status, still serves as the foundation for social ranking. The most respected Malinke are descendants of royalty, followed by nobles, commoners, and an occupational rank of workers and craftsmen. Unlike some African cultures that grant a high level of status to artisans and craftsmen, the Malinke regard these people as lower-class.

Malinke villages consist of several houses that shelter large, extended families. Constructed of woven grass, a traditional Malinke house is round with a cone-shaped roof. More modern houses are built with mud blocks and are square with tin roofs. A typical household has a husband and wife, children, and the husband's parents and grandparents. The eldest male serves as the head of the household and is consulted on all family decisions. Marriages are often arranged by the elders, and brides go to live with their husband's family. At home, women spend most of their time grinding and stor-

A Malinke woman from the former French Guinea.

ing grain, cooking, and caring for the children. A common Malinke meal consists of rice flavored with tomatoes, peppers, and garlic, and a stew called *lakhlalo* that is made from dried fish, vegetables, and a tart fruit called *netetou.*

For the most part, Malinke men are farmers and fishermen. On their fertile land they raise grains, rice, beans, and vegetables. Some of their crops are traded for dairy products such as milk, cheese, and yogurt produced by other cultures. Using canoes carved out of logs, the men also fish in the rivers and mangrove swamps on their land. Some produce colorful cloth and leather goods, which are traded for other food products and tools.

The Malinke are known for their colorful batik and tie-died fabrics used for both women's dresses and men's long, loose-fitting gowns. The fabrics are also made into hunter's shirts, worn by some of the men, which have long slits in the underside of the sleeves for ventilation and several loops sewn into the waist for securing knives. The Malinke who live in cities, such as Bamako and Mali, however, wear Western-style clothing. Gold jewelry, a sign of wealth and status among the Malinke for centuries, is still a popular adornment.

Although most of the Malinke practice Islam, traces of their original religion can also be found. These include ancient customs involving the worship of nature and ancestor spirits.

Dance, considered a Malinke art form, is a focal point of many rituals and often serves as entertainment. Music and folks songs also play an important role in their lives; many Malinke songs have also been adopted by other cultures. Musical instruments such as the xylophone, 21-string harp, and huge drums made from tree trunks create the rhythm and melodies to accompany their songs. These enormous drums were used centuries ago to send messages to neighbors in nearby villages. Today the jeli, the poets from ancient times, serve as folk historians who pass on stories of long ago.

MBUTI
(mm 'boo tee)

POPULATION:	50,000
LOCATION:	Zaire
LANGUAGES:	Mbuti and Efe
PRIMARY FOODS:	Tubers, fruits, yams, corn, fish, snakes, wild boar, monkey, antelope

A SMALL PEOPLE WHO ON AVERAGE STAND BETWEEN FOUR AND five feet tall, the Mbuti live in the Ituri Forest of northeast Zaire and are one of Africa's most well-known cultures. Located on the equator, most of the land they inhabit is in a dense tropical rain forest where the air and soil are always damp.

The people call themselves BaMbuti and are often referred to by others as pygmies. The word *pygmy* is an ancient Greek word that once meant a measure of length from the knuckle to the elbow. It has been used to describe the Mbuti for about 2,000 years.

One of the oldest cultures on the continent, Mbuti ancient history dates back over 3,000 years. Although historians do not know the precise date, Bantu farmers migrated into the Mbuti territory around 2500 B.C. and began trading with them. Primarily hunters and gatherers, the Mbuti welcomed the farm products they received from the Bantu and adopted their Bantu language. They also served as forest guides and soldiers for the Bantus, who chopped down trees and set up villages on the outskirts of the forest. The two cultures have lived harmoniously side by side for centuries.

By the mid-1600s, marriages between the Mbuti and the Bantu farmers were common, and the Mbuti became more and more intermixed with the Bantu. Most of them, however, continued to live in the forests rather than in the Bantu villages.

When European explorers passed through Mbuti territory in the late 1600s, they were fascinated by their way of life, and many began anthropological research on their culture. In the late 1800s, the famed traveler Morton Stanley along with his exploration party got lost in the Ituri Forest; it was the Mbuti who came to their rescue by teaching Stanley and his men how to survive in the rain forest.

Today, most of the Mbuti still live in small forest camps of about 100 people on the outskirts of Bantu villages. These camps function as cooperatives, with all members sharing in the decision-making; no one person serves as a leader or chief. Their dome-shaped huts are made of branches and leaves. Each family has its own hut. Since the Mbuti move from the camps when the surrounding vegetation has been used up, their homes are very simple, as is their clothing. Both men and women go bare chested, wearing only bark or a loincloth wrapped around their hips. Sometimes they wear bracelets made of wood, feathers, or animal teeth, and occasionally

Mbuti man sits by the fire in front of his house in the Ituri Forest, Epulu, Zaire.

they apply red or white dyes to their faces. When performing ceremonial dances, the men wear skirts made of fresh, green leaves. Some of the Mbuti who trade extensively with nearby villagers or have come in contact with Westerners now wear cotton shorts and shirts.

The Mbuti cook their food over an open fire. Typical meals consist of plant roots, wild vegetables, fish, snakes, wild boar, antelope, monkey, or elephant. They also smoke their meat to preserve it for future consumption. Wild honey is eaten on special occasions. In addition to wild meats, they eat yams, corn, fruit, rice, and beans, which they get by trading meat with nearby villagers. They also get tools and cookware from these villagers.

Mbuti family life is based on the belief that men and women are equal. Marriages are monogamous, and intermarriage between relatives is forbidden. If either the husband or the wife is unhappy in their marriage, they can easily dissolve the partnership and choose another mate. Both men and women share in the duties of child rearing, hunting, gathering, and fishing. Many Mbuti families keep a dog for a pet. This breed of dog, called basenji, does not bark and is very useful to the Mbuti during an animal hunt. Having lived in the forest for thousands of years, the Mbuti are very skilled at natural healing. From wild plants they produce medicines that aid headaches, stomachaches, dysentery, and flesh wounds.

Mbuti hunters, Ituri Forest.

Unlike most other African cultures, the Mbuti do not believe in ancestor spirits. Instead they pray to a god they call Molimo (the god of the forest). Many celebrations and festivals honor Molimo. The Mbuti believe that Molimo can intervene on their behalf and punish anyone who does them harm. They also believe that they please their god by living in harmony with the forest.

Although the Mbuti have no paintings, sculptures, or written literature, they do have an array of music, dance, and stories that have been passed down through the centuries. Their music includes the use of flutes and stringed instruments, and their songs are accompanied by the beating of sticks, clapping of hands, and stomping of feet.

While land development and modernization in Zaire have encroached upon the Mbuti territory, for the most part, the Mbuti remain a forest-dwelling people who still practice many of the customs of their ancestors. Few Mbuti children ever attend school, and the people remain a small ethnic minority in the country.

NDEBELE
(nn day 'bay lay)

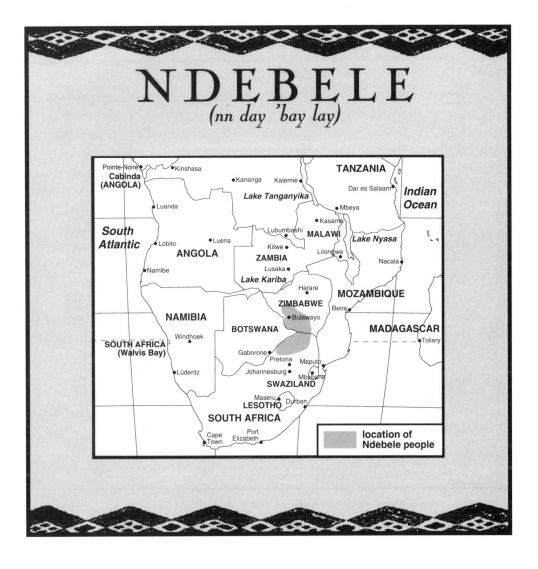

POPULATION:	2,500,000
LOCATION:	Zimbabwe, South Africa
LANGUAGES:	Ndebele, English
PRIMARY FOODS:	Maize, cereals, sour milk, vegetables, eggs, beef, turtle

THE NDEBELE, OR AMANDEBELE AS THEY PREFER TO CALL THEM-
selves, once belonged to the vast Zulu kingdom. Their name
is a Sotho (the language of Lesotho) word meaning
"stranger." The majority of the Ndebele live in the southern African
country of Zimbabwe (formerly Rhodesia), and a smaller group resides in the country of South Africa. For the most part, the Ndebele
in Zimbabwe inhabit the southwestern high plains regions of the
country. The land, with an average elevation of 4,500 feet, ranges
from grassy fields to rocky hills and lies between the Zambezi River
basin to the north and the Limpopo River basin to the south.

Once a powerful kingdom that ruled over much of the territory
that is now Zimbabwe, the Ndebele were keen warriors who resisted
domination by other peoples. Their history as an independent people began in the early 1800s, when, led by Chief Mzilikazi, they
broke away from the oppressive power of the then-reigning Zulu
king. Most of the breakaway members left the Zulu land and moved
to the wooded uplands of Zimbabwe; a few headed southward to
the present-day area of Pretoria in South Africa. Once rooted in
their new territories, they established themselves as the kingdom of
Matabele (the Sotho pronunciation of the word) and gained control
of much of the land that had belonged to the Shona tribe already
living in the area. Eventually most of the Ndebele in South Africa
moved northward to Zimbabwe in the late 1830s.

During the 1890s, the British colonizers in Zimbabwe began to
spread out amid Ndebele territory in search of gold, diamonds, and
elephant tusks. After renaming the country Rhodesia, the British,
with their European gun power, became a formidable enemy of the
Ndebele. They confiscated their land and livestock, confined them
to reserves of barren land, subjected them to unfair taxation, disallowed them from attending schools, and forced them to work in
labor camps. In the late 1890s tensions escalated between the British
and the Ndebele, who deeply resented their domination, and in the
years that followed a series of confrontations took place between the
two. In 1896 the Ndebele rebelled, and a bloody battle left many of
the British dead. But the situation would remain bleak for decades
to come.

It wasn't until the 1970s, when black power movements in-
stilled a sense of pride and right to self-determination in Africa, that

Ndebele houses near the Bembesi River in Zimbabwe, 1947.

Ndebele beadwork motifs from South Africa.

things began to change for the Ndebele. Although they had had territorial problems with the native Shona peoples in the past, the two decided to join forces and fight against colonial rule. Finally, in 1980, the country gained independence and became the Republic of Zimbabwe.

Although most of the Ndebele now live in Zimbabwe, they are a minority in the country. Their numbers equal only 14 percent of the population, whereas the Shona represent 80 percent. Within the Zimbabwe political system, conflicts between the Shona and the Ndebele still exist.

Today, the Ndebele are ranked within their own society by a hierarchy of classes. The *Zanzi* upper class are descendants of the original group of Ndebele who broke free from the Zulus. The *Enhla* middle class are descendants of groups conquered by the Ndebele during their growth period. And the *Holi* lower class are descendants of those who voluntarily joined with the Ndebele. Despite the existence of the class system, many Ndebele intermarry across the classes.

A few chiefs still govern over Ndebele provinces, but in recent years their authority has waned. Most of the Ndebele rebelled against the political and economic control the chiefs once had over them, and now regard national governments as their authorities.

A few Ndebele still live as hunters and farmers, but the tradition is quickly fading. Most grow just enough food for their own families. The once common thatch-roof houses are also becoming a thing of the past, replaced by cement structures with bold graphic designs painted on the exteriors. Many of the Ndebele are employed in industrial sectors, mining for gold and gems, and producing steel, textiles, and appliances. Some of them live and work in the cities during the week and commute home to the rural areas for weekends. A few work as farmhands for white landowners.

The extended family is the foundation for homelife. Some men still maintain more than one wife, but the practice of polygamy is not as prevalent as it was years ago. Although infidelity in marriage is acceptable for husbands, it is forbidden for wives. Women caught having extramarital affairs are usually divorced by their husbands and lose the right to see their children.

Child rearing is a shared responsibility, and Ndebele custom dictates two mothers for each child: the natural or "little" mother, and a "big" mother who is an older woman capable of raising the child should a family crisis arise (similar to the Christian custom of naming a godparent for a newborn child). This dual-mother system ensures all children of a stable upbringing, and no distinctions are made between biological relationships and social ones. Even the breast-feeding of babies is shared among nursing women in case one woman's milk supply runs dry.

A typical meal for the Ndebele consists of a thick porridge made from maize, complemented with sour milk and wild green vegetables. Other common foods include cornmeal stew, roasted turtle steaks, raw hens' eggs, caterpillars and insects, and sun-dried,

Ndebele painted wall design from South Africa.

salt-cured, or freshly slaughtered raw meats. Monkey meat, which is eaten by some African cultures, is forbidden by Ndebele custom.

Although some of the Ndebele converted to Christianity during the British colonial rule, most still practice many of their older religious customs. An important element of these customs is the use of priestesses—older women who are thought to be prophets. These priestesses, called *igosos,* channel information between the Ndebele and their spirit ancestors, who in turn pass the prayers and wishes on to the Ndebele high god known as Nkulunkulu. And although the Zimbabwe government has implemented a public health system, many of the people still call on natural healers who use herbs and rituals to rid them of poor health.

Most of the Ndebele have given up their traditional leather robes in favor of more Western-style clothing. Also rare are the distinctive rows of copper rings worn around the necks, arms, and ankles of Ndebele women. And the once common Ndebele initiation right of slitting earlobes has all but disappeared. Almost all Ndebele children now attend government schools, where classes are taught in English. But Zimbabwe has a severe teacher shortage, and educational opportunities at the upper levels are scarce.

SAN
(sahn)

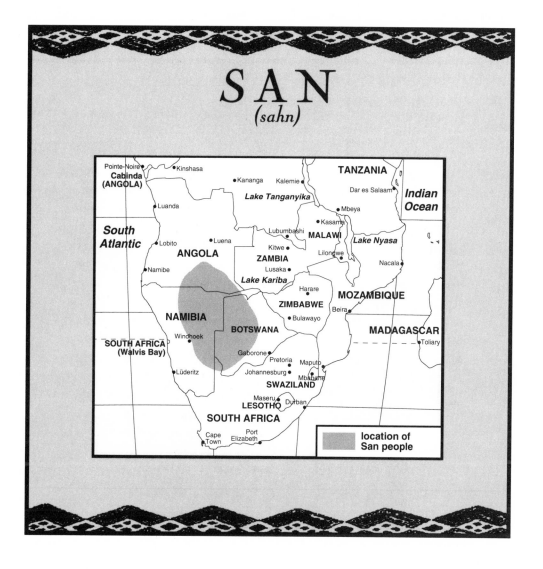

Pointe-Noire
Kinshasa
Cabinda
(ANGOLA)
Kananga
Kalemie
TANZANIA
Lake Tanganyika
Dar es Salaam
**Indian
Ocean**
Luanda
Mbeya
**South
Atlantic**
Lobito
Luena
Lubumbashi
MALAWI
Lake Nyasa
Kasama
Namibe
ANGOLA
Kitwe
Lilongwe
Nacala
ZAMBIA
Lusaka
Lake Kariba
Harare
MOZAMBIQUE
NAMIBIA
ZIMBABWE
Beira
Windhoek
BOTSWANA
Bulawayo
MADAGASCAR
SOUTH AFRICA
(Walvis Bay)
Toliary
Gaborone
Pretoria
Maputo
Lüderitz
Johannesburg
Mbabane
SWAZILAND
Maseru
Durban
LESOTHO
SOUTH AFRICA
Cape
Town
Port
Elizabeth

location of
San people

POPULATION:	55,000
LOCATION:	Namibia, Botswana, and Angola
LANGUAGE:	Khoisan
PRIMARY FOODS:	Roots, tubers, berries, fruit, nuts, wild game

LTHOUGH IT IS BELIEVED THAT THE SAN ONCE ROAMED ALL OF southern Africa from the Cape of Good Hope to Zimbabwe, Angola, and Mozambique, over the course of several hundred years they have been driven out of the well-watered grasslands and scrub forests and into the Kalahari Desert. Remarkably, they are well adapted to the harsh conditions of life in the arid desert wasteland, where midday temperatures can reach as high as 140 degrees Fahrenheit.

The San are a unique racial group, differing from other African peoples, and it has been suggested by some anthropologists that they have Asian ancestry. They are small in stature, the men not more than five feet, two inches tall, with loose yellow skin able to reflect substantially more sunlight than the skin of other dark-skinned Africans.

About 2,000 San continue to live a semitraditional life in the

These San rock engravings (above and left) are from the lower Riet River,
Cape Province, South Africa.

San rock painting depicting two mythical creatures, from the Tsibab ravine in South-West Africa.

eastern Kalahari Desert, under the protection of a United Nations foundation. These San travel hundreds of square miles on foot over the Kalahari in search of game or roots and fruits for their diet. They move in small nomadic bands related by blood and marriage ties, each group having its own territory, which might be several hundred square miles in size. They have contact with one another through trade, visitation, and marriage, but they are not politically organized. Although they all share the click group of languages, distinguished by short pops and clicks made with the tongue in various parts of the mouth, there are variations and differing dialects among bands. Today, as the resources of the Kalahari are depleted, San find it increasingly difficult to preserve their traditional way of life.

San dwellings are small, dome-shaped grass *scherms* erected wherever they stop to make camp. In dry months, they may simply dig holes in the ground and fill them with straw for sleeping, marking each bed with a stick to let others know not to cross it and thus disturb the spirits that rest with the family.

San possessions are few and simple. Ostrich eggs and ani-

San rock painting of a mythical creature, from
Mashonaland, Rhodesia.

mal stomachs are used for collecting and storing water; leather
sacks, for carrying bows and small bone arrows. Everything is shared
in order to preserve the trust and cooperation so necessary
to survival.

Women wear a leather apron in front and sometimes also in the
rear. A cloak called a *kaross* is tied on the right shoulder with a
leather thong and passed under the left arm. A pouch can be formed
in the kaross to carry a baby or food gathered at the veld. Women
also wear jewelry, and their aprons are usually edged with ostrich
eggshell beads. Pieces of ostrich egg may also be strung and worn in
their hair or as a bracelet. Sometimes a tortoise shell is hung around
the neck. This shell is plugged with beeswax, then filled with an
aromatic powdered root that is applied to the neck with a soft piece
of leather.

San men wear simple leather thongs and occasionally leather

A San village in West Africa.

sandals. All men have an initiation mark between the eyebrows and
stripes on their shoulders and backs. These marks are tiny rows of
scars made with a sharp instrument, meant to resemble the stripes
of a zebra.

The hard conditions of the desert require that the San travel in
small groups. Families must also be small, or it would be impossible
to support them. Marriages are monogamous within a patriarchal
society, and despite the small size of families, the aged and infirm
are cared for rather than abandoned. Women give birth alone, away
from the camp. In times of extreme hardship, the San practice infan-

ticide—babies who are born crippled or sick are killed because they would be too much of a burden.

San are essentially hunter-gatherers. Their diet consists of berries, fruits, tubers, and roots collected in the desert. They are also skillful hunters, shooting their prey—antelope, springbok, eland, or wildebeest—with bows and arrows dipped in a mixture of animal and vegetable poisons. They must then track the wounded prey across the veld until it falls and can be killed with a spear. The animal is immediately butchered, and nothing is wasted. They dry the meat, drink the blood, and even squeeze out the stomach to collect the liquid for drinking. Once the bones have been cracked and the marrow eaten, they are made into arrows. The skin is saved for clothing.

Spiritual practices place great emphasis on the dead, who are thought to possess supernatural powers. The San believe that the spirit of a man stays with his people. When a San dies, the body is buried in an upright, sitting position. Arms are crossed over the chest, the legs are folded with the knees drawn up, and the ankles are tied together. The head is placed in a resting position on top of updrawn fists. The body is then wrapped in an old kaross and placed in the deep grave. Each member of the band throws a ritual handful of dirt into the grave to ensure a peaceful departure of the spirit and that each will be remembered. Finally, the grave is filled and covered with thorn branches to protect it from scavengers.

San worship the moon as well as the stars. Most of their prayers are for food, and most of their dances imitate the animals they hunt. Their legends often celebrate their own abilities, the heroes being small animals like jackals who manage to survive through wit and cunning while larger animals like lions are killed. Evidence that the San once had a highly developed artistic tradition can be found in the many rock and cave paintings that still exist, most notably in South-West Africa.

Most San have undergone radical changes in their lives in recent years; those who adhere to the traditional way of life are a dwindling minority. Many San have had to take jobs as household servants and on farms bordering the desert in order to survive. One such group lives in present-day Namibia. During the time that the South West Africa People's Organization (SWAPO) challenged white control of Namibia, the South African military built camps in the San's area and hired the San as trackers and camp workers. When South Africa withdrew from Namibia, the San were afraid that the new government would punish them as collaborators; about 3,000 San followed the soldiers home to South Africa.

Some of the San in Namibia today receive help with their farming from the Namibian government and the United Nations World Food Program. Although some of the San are adjusting to more modern ways of life, progress is slow, and only a minuscule number of San children ever get the chance to have a formal education.

TSWANA

('tswa nah)

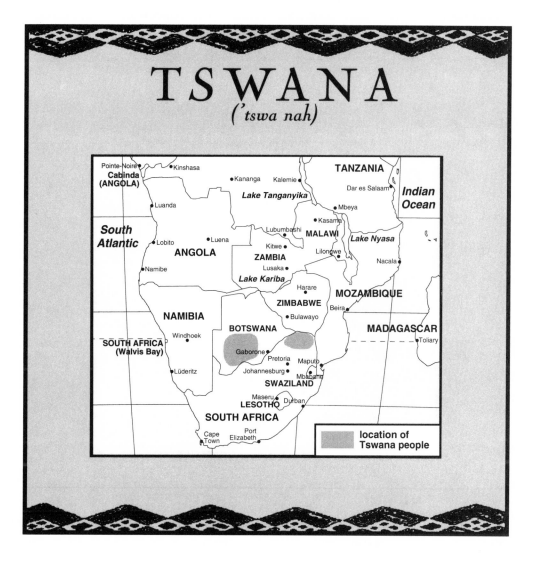

location of Tswana people

POPULATION:	3,000,000
LOCATION:	Botswana, South Africa
LANGUAGES:	Setswana, English
PRIMARY FOODS:	Millet, maize, beans, squash, melons, dried meat, beer

A SUBGROUP OF THE SOTHO PEOPLES, THE TSWANA THROUGH the years have conquered and absorbed many other cultures. Two-thirds of the Tswana population lives in South Africa, in one of the largest black territories in the country; the remaining one-third reside in Botswana—"land of the Tswana," where the strongest presence of Tswana culture can be found.

In South Africa, the Tswana territory is called Bophuthatswana. The land is so depleted and dry that most of the Tswana must work in white-controlled areas of survive. In Botswana, the Tswana live in the Kalahari Basin, another dry region with pockets of scrub bushes and tree savannas. Here the climate changes with the season; temperatures range from 100 degrees Fahrenheit in the summer to below freezing in winter. Most of the Tswana live in rural areas near the South Africa and Zimbabwe borders, where the land is more suitable for farming.

The history of the Tswana dates back to the 14th century, when the Sotho peoples in the Transvaal region of southern Africa began breaking up into several groups. Warring among the chiefs' relatives and poor farming conditions caused the groups to find other places to live. By the 17th century, several Tswana groups settled in the eastern regions of Botswana.

During the early 1800s, members of other groups, such as the Ndebele and the Khoisan, joined the Tswana, almost doubling their total population. By the late 1880s, Dutch, French, and German settlers had penetrated much of the Tswana land, and many Tswana converted to Christianity. When gold and diamonds were discovered in the area during the late 1800s, the settlers made life difficult for the Tswana by levying taxes on their land and forcing them to work for the new landowners. Although Botswana by this time was a British Protectorate, Tswana chiefs tried to preserve their culture and negotiated with the British in an effort to limit their control. In 1966, under the leadership of Tswana chief Seretse Khama, Botswana gained its independence from the British, and in the following years it managed to maintain a stable democratic government. Following Khama's death in 1980, another Tswana, Sir Ketumite Masire, replaced him as president and continues to govern the country.

Today, about 90 percent of the Botswana population is Tswana, but few of these are direct descendants of the original members who

Tswana beadwork belt motif from Botswana.

left the Sotho people. Although poor farming conditions have forced many of the Tswana to migrate to cities such as Gaborone and Serowe, most still live in the quiet rural areas of the south. A small percentage of them work in the mining industries—diamonds, copper, iron, lead, nickel, coal—that support most of the country. Some of the Tswana find temporary employment as migrant workers in South Africa. Primary school education is common, but secondary education is still insufficient to meet the needs of the population. High illiteracy rates among the Tswana have kept most of them in agriculture or low-paying jobs. Those who reside in South Africa live in the Tswana territory north of Johannesburg. Like most blacks in South Africa, they see the election of Nelson Mandela and the dismantling of apartheid as signifying the possibility for a better life.

A pattern repeated on the inside of a Tswana woven basket from Botswana.

A Tswana bead apron design from Botswana.

Most Tswana houses are modern structures made of wood, concrete block, and glass, with many modern European conveniences such as electrical appliances. A few of the traditional houses, made of dried mud with cone-shaped thatch roofs, can still be found in rural areas. Traditional styles of dress are a thing of the past, replaced by Western-style clothing.

In a typical Tswana household, duties are divided between the men and the women, but the women do a larger share of the work. They repair the homes; produce pottery and baskets; cook; clean; and collect food, water, and firewood. The men hunt and raise cattle and act as the head of the household.

The diet of the Tswana is varied. Millet and maize serve as staples, along with beans, peas, and squash. When in season, melons and berries are consumed. Spicy chutneys are used to liven up ordinary meals. The Tswana also eat beef, lamb, and pork (which they raise on their land) and the meat of hunted wild animals. To preserve the meat for times of shortage, they salt it and dry it in the sun. A favorite beverage is a milky beer called *bojalwa,* which is made by the women from sorghum and millet.

Both Christianity, adopted during colonial times, and the original Tswana religious customs are practiced. Although Tswana custom allows for men to have more than one wife, the Christian influence during the 1800s lessened this practice. The belief in ancestor spirits and spirits in objects in nature is common, and farmers occasionally perform rain dances with the hope of helping their crops. Although government health clinics have been established in both Botswana and South Africa, many Tswana still seek the advice of natural healers who use herbal medicines to cure their ills.

TUAREG
('twa reg)

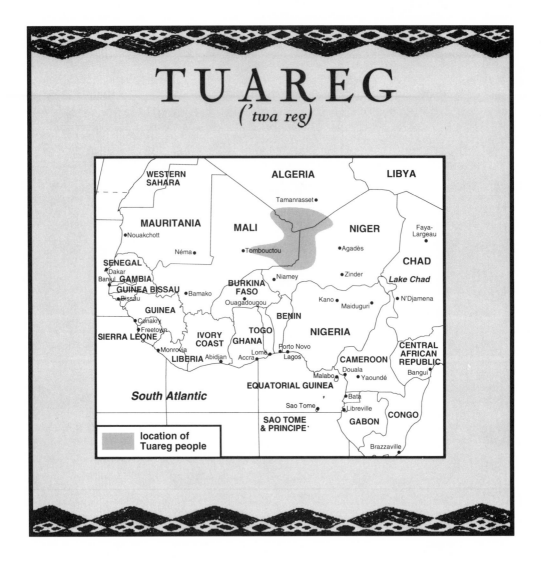

location of
Tuareg people

POPULATION:	400,000
LOCATION:	Algeria, Mali, and Niger
LANGUAGES:	Tamahaq, Arabic
PRIMARY FOODS:	Milk from camels, goats, and sheep; millet; dates; meat from sheep and goats

KNOWN AS THE "PEOPLE OF THE VEIL," THE TUAREG LIVE IN THE area of Africa where the borders of Algeria, Mali, and Niger converge. This region includes a mountain range in Niger, as well as the Ahaggar Mountains of southern Algeria, the Tassili Plateau, and the territory north and immediately south of the great bend of the Niger River. The terrain includes both savanna and steppe regions, and in the central northern area mountain peaks tower over a desert. In adapting to the sandstorms of the desert, the Tuareg traders and raiders of the past would cover their faces with veils, earning them the name "warriors of the blue veil." In contrast to this desert area, the region they inhabit in the south receives 10–20 inches of rainfall per year, making it suitable for the cultivation of crops such as bullrush millet.

Originating in northeastern Africa, the Tuareg, along with the Berbers, took up camel raising between A.D. 100 and 500. This enabled them to expand across the Sahara to the edges of the West Africa savanna. Following a series of migrations that probably began

Tuareg men riding camels in Mali, near Timbuktu.

in the seventh century, the Tuareg spread out across the southwestern parts of the desert all the way to Timbuktu. Along with camel herding, they became the leading traders of ivory, gold, copper, and slaves. The Tuareg were influenced by Bedouin Arabs with whom they came into contact, and adopted the Muslim faith. Although they retain some vestiges of their earlier Christian faith—their favorite decorative motif is the cross—for the most part, the Tuareg have abandoned their ancestral way of life and have adopted that of the Muslims.

Tuareg man wearing pounded indigo cloth.

Several events in the history of the Tuareg contributed to a division within the culture. Starting in the late 19th century, the French moved in, claiming the desert as a colonial possession. The Tuareg resisted but were eventually defeated. Then, during a religious war in 1917, the Tuareg were driven out of the mountain region, and many were killed. The survivors fled to various other areas, including villages in Niger and Nigeria where they began to take up a more settled life especially following the severe droughts of the early 1970s. Although many Tuareg resumed the herding life with the return of normal rainfall, there remains a division. Those Tuareg living closer to villages around the Niger River have become farmers who trade their crops for salt from the desert-dwelling Tuareg.

Tuareg social structure is stratified, that is, a caste system prevails, ranging from nobles and vassals to *Inanden* (workers). There are several types of workers: sheep herders, goat herders, camel

Tuareg woman pounding grain in Mali.

herders, leather workers, farmers, and ironsmiths. Herders are more respected than farmers. There is also a lower caste of servants, called the *Iklan,* who were subjugated by the clan years ago, and who work for minimal pay and are akin to slaves. A further social structure exists in the division of the Tuareg into seven groups under seven chiefs. The chief, or *Amenskal,* has authority only with the permission of the people, and the people refer to themselves as *Imuhar* (free men).

The Tuareg who continue in their traditional herding and trading lifestyle survive by transporting goods between trucks and railcars, as well as carrying goods to places that are inaccessible to trucks. These nomadic Tuareg still construct the traditional tents as shelter. Made of tanned animal skins that have been dyed red, the Tuareg tents stand out from the cloth tents erected by the Arab Bedouins with whom the Tuareg had very early contact. The farming Tuareg construct homes of grass or mat, bound together with ropes. Some Tuareg have gone to live in the cities, where they work as laborers in the port communities of Nigeria and Ghana.

Clothing of the Tuareg remains mostly traditional. Men wear loose-fitting trousers and poncho-style cotton shirts. Women wear the same type of shirts, as well as shawls and sandals. When meeting with strangers, some Tuareg men still cover their faces with a veil, lifting it only to eat or drink. Unlike most other Muslim societies, Tuareg women cover their mouths with cloth but do not wear veils. Those Tuareg who live in cities, however, have abandoned the use of veils and have adopted a Western style of dress.

The diet of both groups of Tuareg remains similar. They use the milk of their camels, sheep, and goats. Meat comes from the sheep and goats. These products, along with salt from the desert, are traded with the farming Tuareg for millet and sweet, sun-dried dates.

The division of labor is somewhat traditional: Men do the farming, herding, and building of the houses; and women take care of the children and households. The existence of the lower-caste labor force, however, has provided many of the women with the opportunity to pursue the arts, in particular poetry and music. Reading and writing are more common among Tuareg women than men. A common Tuareg event called an *ahal* is a celebration where the women tell stories and recite poetry. The men usually sit still during ahal, peering through their veils with great respect for the women. In general, Tuareg women are highly regarded.

Unlike other Muslim peoples, the Tuareg men take just one wife, and fidelity in marriage is considered sacred. A woman is only allowed to marry a man from her own or a higher caste, whereas a man has to marry a women from his own or a lower caste. A typical Tuareg family consists of a husband, wife, children, and relatives from both the husband's and wife's family. Daughters as well as sons inherit the family wealth, land, and livestock.

The Tuareg are known throughout Africa for their beautifully crafted leather belts and sacks that are usually produced by the women. They are also known for having created their own alphabet and peculiar script characters that were derived from a Libyan alphabet of the fourth century.

TUTSI

('toot see)

CHAD
SUDAN
• Berbera
• Addis Ababa
CENTRAL
AFRICAN REPUBLIC
• Wau
ETHIOPIA
CAMEROON
• Juba
Lake Turkana
SOMALIA
Bangui •
Lake Albert
UGANDA
KENYA
Kisangani •
Kampala •
Lake Victoria
• Mogadishu
CONGO
• Nairobi
GABON
ZAIRE
RWANDA
Kigali •
BURUNDI
Bujumbura •
Brazzaville •
• Kinshasa
TANZANIA
Mombasa•
Indian
Ocean
• Kananga
Kalemie •
Dar es Salaam•
• Luanda
Lake Tanganyika
• Mbeya
• Kasama
• Lobito
• Luena
Lubumbashi •
MALAWI
Lake Nyasa
Kitwe •
ANGOLA
ZAMBIA
Lilongwe •
Nacala •
MADAGASCAR
• Namibe
Lusaka •
Mahajanga
Harare •
MOZAMBIQUE
Antananarivo •
ZIMBABWE

location of
Tutsi people

POPULATION:	690,000
LOCATION:	Rwanda and Burundi
LANGUAGES:	Rwand and Rundi
PRIMARY FOODS:	Dairy products including milk and butter, beans, bananas, cassava, meat

A PEOPLE WHOSE HISTORY OF WEALTH AND POWER STILL BRINGS them pride today, the Tutsi, or Batutsi as many of them call themselves, live in the highlands of east-central Africa, an area with elevations that range from 4,000 feet in the valleys to 9,000 feet in the mountains. The terrain is varied and very rugged, including swamps, rivers, lakes, and mountain ranges. Although rainfall averages 40–50 inches per year, it is unpredictable and at times so heavy that it erodes the topsoil. At high elevations the temperature drops below freezing; at lower elevations the weather can be extremely hot and humid.

Although ancient Tutsi myths link the culture to peoples of Egypt and Ethiopia, more scholarly sources trace their history to the 14th century in the east-central African land of modern-day Rwanda and Burundi. At that time, the Tutsi were cattle herders who subjugated the Hutu, an agricultural society living within the same region. Once the Hutu were subdued by the Tutsi, an interdependent system known as *ubuhake* was established. Within this system, the Hutu produced agricultural products and cared for the cattle herds, which remained the property of the Tutsi. They also had to pay taxes to the Tutsi king, or *mwami*. In return, the Hutu were protected by their masters. This ubuhake system enabled wealth and power to reside with the Tutsi.

Along with ubuhake, a caste system developed. Within the society, the uppermost or ruling caste are called *Batutsi* and are descendants of the original cattle herders. They resemble lighter-skinned people from the Nile region and control most of the wealth and power. The middle caste are the *Bahuti,* descendants of the Hutu. The Bahuti care for the cattle and crops and make up the majority of the population. The lower caste are the *Batwa,* who like the Hutu were once subjugated by the Tutsi. The Batwa are the hunters, foragers, and pottery makers. Each caste group member has a loyalty to fellow caste members, along with a loyalty to the entire Tutsi society.

Like many other African cultures, the Tutsi experienced a period of European colonization. The Germans took charge in the late 1890s and ceded authority to the Belgians in the 1940s, who tried to wipe out ubuhake in order to weaken the power of the Tutsi king. Throughout the 1950s, the Tutsi were granted positions of authority within the Belgian government, along with powerful positions in ed-

Elite Tutsi dancers, called *Ntore,* perform on the shore of Lake Kivu, in Goma, Zaire.

ucation and other professions. This inequality further increased friction between the Tutsi and Hutu people and led to a Hutu rebellion in 1959. In 1961 the Belgian government granted independence to Rwanda and Burundi. In Rwanda, the Hutu overpowered the Tutsi and seized control of the government. In Burundi, the Tutsi remained in power until 1993, when Melchior Ndadaye toppled the Tutsi government and was elected as the country's first Hutu president.

Although not as strict as it was in the past, the social structure of the Tutsi today still revolves around the caste system. People inherit the position and occupation of their ancestors and are expected to marry a person from their own caste. Family life is organized into groups who trace their descent to a common ancestor. These family groups are called *inzu* and are very important in maintaining the rituals of marriage, tax paying, and even feuding with other family groups. Usually, they consist of at least five generations of one family. Families in rural areas live in an interconnected, enclosed compound containing separate buildings for the family, servants,

Sewn pattern on a Tutsi matting screen
from Rwanda.

reception hall, and kitchen. Some common Tutsi meals include bananas fried with green peas, stewed cassava and pinto beans, and
ground beef seasoned with ginger and curry.

Marriages are based on traditional gender roles and expecta-
tions. Grooms ideally possess many cattle, and brides should be
good housekeepers as well as basket weavers. Proper mates are
often chosen by a person's family to ensure that the inzu remains a
tightly connected unit. Although children once got instruction in
gender roles at home, today they receive a school-based education.
At an early age, children are taught to be obedient and respectful of
their elders and are responsible for minor chores.

The religious practices of the Tutsi are a combination of Christianity, which was adopted during colonial times, and old Bantu customs. They believe in several gods and in spirits of the dead who are
often evil tempered. Sometimes the Tutsi construct a special hut as
a sign of respect for male ancestors. Women often sit in the huts as
a way of providing a peace offering to the spirits. Other values em-
braced by the Tutsi include loyalty, trustworthiness, courage, and
self-control.

The Tutsi practice various art forms. Storytelling, once an important part of a man's preparation for becoming a warrior, is still
an important means of passing on their history and a pleasurable
pastime. Tutsi men are also very good at reciting poetry. Dancing
has held an important place in Tutsi society both as preparation for
a hunt and in ceremonies that reenact the event. Tutsi women make
beautiful jewelry of geometrically woven beadwork, which is worn as
headdresses, bracelets, and necklaces. They also produce intricately
woven baskets.

Although some of the Tutsi still follow an agricultural way of
life, many now live in urban areas and have adopted a Western life-

style. For the most part, the 400-year-old system of ubuhake has been wiped out, but the ongoing rivalries between the Tutsi and the Hutu continue to create tensions in both Burundi and Rwanda today. In 1994 the presidents of Burundi and Rwanda—both Hutus—were killed when a plane in which they were flying was shot down by Tutsi supporters. The event sparked a savage ethnic war between the two groups, and in the following months hundreds of thousands of Tutsis and Hutus were killed in Burundi and Rwanda. The brutal killings caused many Tutsi to flee both Burundi and Rwanda and seek refuge in neighboring countries. This long-lasting rivalry, along with environmental problems and the loss of cattle, has made it difficult to achieve national ethnic unity in Burundi and Rwanda.

WOLOF
('waw lawf)

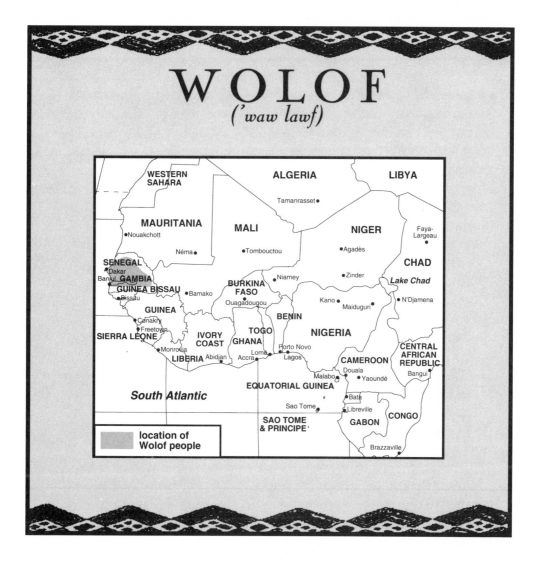

WESTERN SAHARA

ALGERIA

LIBYA

Tamanrasset●

MAURITANIA

●Nouakchott

MALI

Néma●

●Tombouctou

NIGER

Faya-Largeau●

Agadès●

CHAD

SENEGAL

Dakar

Banjul GAMBIA

GUINEA BISSAU

●Bissau

Bamako●

Niamey●

Zinder●

Lake Chad

●N'Djamena

GUINEA

Conakry●

Freetown

SIERRA LEONE

Monrovia●

LIBERIA Abidjan●

IVORY COAST

BURKINA FASO

Ouagadougou●

Kano● Maiduguri●

BENIN

TOGO

GHANA

Accra●

Porto Novo

Lomé●

Lagos●

NIGERIA

CAMEROON

Douala●

Malabo●

●Yaoundé

CENTRAL AFRICAN REPUBLIC

Bangui●

South Atlantic

EQUATORIAL GUINEA

Sao Tome●

●Bata

●Libreville

CONGO

SAO TOME & PRINCIPE·

GABON

Brazzaville●

location of Wolof people

POPULATION:	1,300,000
LOCATION:	Senegal, Gambia
LANGUAGES:	Wolof, French, and English
PRIMARY FOODS:	Millet, peppers, pumpkins, beans, fruit, nuts, fish, meat

THE WOLOF ARE PRIMARILY AN AGRICULTURAL PEOPLE WHO SET-tled in the savanna grasslands located between the Senegal River and the Gambia River in the extreme west of Africa. In the low, coastal area that rises gently to a plateau, the average elevation is approximately 1,000 feet above sea level. Rainfall varies from a yearly average of 20 inches in the immediate area to 80 or more inches near the southwestern region of Casamance. Farther east, the land is subject to long, dry spells, and Wolof farmers are at risk of losing their crops to drought.

It is possible that the Wolof originally came from the north before settling in the area. The first king, Ndiadiane N'diaye, was in power during the late 14th century. His empire included a number of states, each having its own ruler. By the 15th century the Wolof had conquered most of the ethnic groups in the region.

By the time the Portuguese arrived seeking slaves in the late 1400s, the rulers had joined together to form a college of electors. They chose the *burba,* or supreme king, while retaining power over their own territories. When Wolof Prince Bemoi, who ruled during the 1480s, tried to pursue greater unity among his people, the rulers rebelled, contributing to the downfall of the empire.

In 1673 the Fulani waged a holy war against the Wolof king-doms and began to convert them to Islam. At the time, the policies of the Wolof ruler, who was growing wealthy from trading ivory and slaves to the Portuguese, were particularly oppressive, and Islam and its leaders appeared more desirable to the Wolof people.

When the French arrived in the late 1800s to settle an island off the coast of Wolof country, they soon began to expand into Wolof territory. In 1895, the region became a colony of French West Africa, and the Wolof were granted French citizenship. In 1960 the French granted independence to Senegal, and in 1965 the British granted independence to Gambia. Although they make up the bulk of the population in Senegal, the Wolof do not have much political power in the country.

Today the once-agricultural Wolof reside in both cities and countryside. Some of them live in mixed villages with other cultures. Villages are made up of a group of houses arranged around an open square often containing a raised platform that serves as a meeting place for the men. Houses are constructed of mud or reed walls and

This postcard from the 1890s shows a young Wolof man from Senegal wearing gold jewelry.

thatched, conical-shaped roofs. A few pieces of furniture such as prayer mats and beds may be placed inside. City homes are usually built a few feet off the ground, have a cement floor, a corrugated metal roof, and a porch.

The division of labor between men and women is clearly defined. Wolof men clear the land, raise the crops, weave baskets and mats, build houses, perform music, teach religion, and conduct trade. Women handle household duties, take care of children, draw water, sell excess crops, and gather medicinal plants. Wolof who live in urban areas, such as Dakar and Banjul, work as merchants, teachers, fishermen, and government officials.

Marriages among the Wolof are usually arranged by the groom's parents, who consider first cousins on the father's side of the family to be the best choices. Occasionally, a young man who wishes to marry a certain young woman without his parents' consent may seek the advice of a fortune-teller to determine their compatibility. Once a bride is chosen, a bride-price is set and a Muslim wedding ceremony is planned. This bride-price is considered compensation for the pain of childbirth, and if a wife does not produce children, she is expected to return the bride-price to her husband's family. In very religious families, the bride does not attend her own wedding ceremony. At some wedding ceremonies children are dressed in the clothes of the opposite sex.

As in other Muslim societies, a man may take more than one wife as long as he can provide a private room in his home for her and support her. Older wives will often choose a younger wife for their husbands and take on the responsibility of initiating her into their household. All new wives are expected to show respect for their husband's first wife, who holds supreme status in the family.

The main staple of the Wolof diet is millet. In the morning, millet is served mixed with sour milk, fruit, and sugar. For the evening meal, it is ground into a flour, steamed, and served with leafy vegetables, pumpkin, peppers, beans, and sometimes meat or fish in a dish called *chere*.

A postcard labeled "A Young Girl from Cayor" shows a Wolof girl from Senegal, circa 1910.

The Wolof practice a mixture of ancient African beliefs and the Muslim religion they adopted in the 17th century. Small mosques are important gathering centers in most villages. In the Baol region of central Senegal, a grand Wolof mosque receives hundreds of thousands of visitors each year. Wolof boys are given religious instruction including lessons from the Koran beginning at age seven. Remnants of their ancient religion include the belief in sorcerers, ancestor spirits, an imaginary snake that causes death, and midgets who protect wild animals. To ward off evil spirits, the Wolof often wear amulets that contain passages from the Koran.

A Wolof bridal party, Gambia, 1950.

A wide variety of arts and crafts are created by the Wolof, but craftspeople in general are considered low in social status. The women make pottery, bowls, water jars, and pots out of sun-dried clay. The men make beautiful filigree jewelry of gold and silver. Wolof leather workers make goods for sale to Europeans, such as handbags, wallets, and sandals.

The Wolof are also known for their dancing, drumming, wrestling, singing, and storytelling. *Griots* are singers who recite family histories in song verse, use riddles and fables to entertain children, deliver news and messages, and make speeches on important issues. These days the griots perform on radio stations as well as in small villages.

Today, the Wolof in Gambia are a minority and represent only 14 percent of the population. In Senegal they are the largest ethnic group in the country and make up over 35 percent of the population. Since 1980, Abdou Diof, a member of the Wolof, has served as president.

YORUBA

('yawr uh buh)

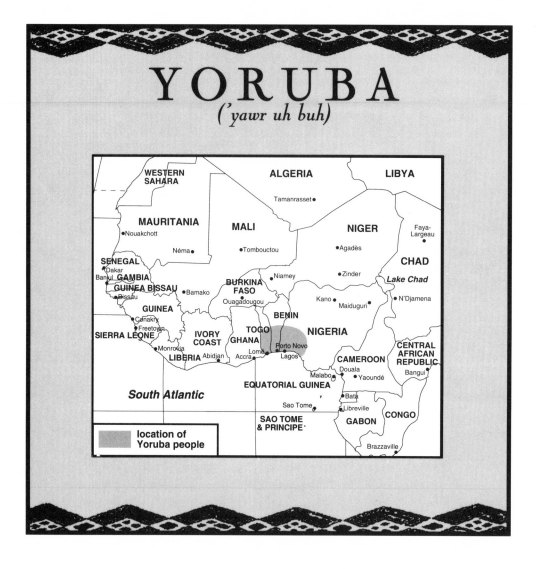

location of
Yoruba people

POPULATION:	17,000,000
LOCATION:	Nigeria, Benin, Togo
LANGUAGE:	Yoruba
PRIMARY FOODS:	Beans, yams, bananas, maize, cassava, fish, palm oil soup, meat

FOR THOUSANDS OF YEARS, THE YORUBA HAVE OCCUPIED THE territory that today falls in the southwestern area of Nigeria and crosses the border extending into neighboring Benin and Togo. Rainfall along the coast is heavy, about 80 inches a year, but the soil is poor in this area of both dense forests and swamps. To the north, however, there are good agricultural conditions, moderate rainfall, and rich soil. There is also a belt of deciduous forest extending through the northwest, and it is in this forest that the "Ile of Ife," the cultural and spiritual center of the Yoruba, is located.

Although no written record exists of Yoruba history prior to contact with Europeans, their oral legends, as well as modern language and archaeological studies, provide strong evidence that the Yoruba have occupied their homeland for thousands of years. According to a Yoruba creation myth, they are descended from Oduduwa, the creator, who came down from heaven on an iron chain and established a city in the Ile of Ife, and whose 16 sons went out to form their own kingdoms.

By the 11th century the Yoruba had established a sophisticated culture that dominated several large cities, including Ife, Oyo, and Benin. These urban centers contained palaces, central courtyards, and a high wall surrounding the entire city. By the 1600s, their empire was vast, and their political and economic control stretched for hundreds of miles. However, the Yoruba experienced

The Timi of Ede, John Adetoyese Laoye I, a Yoruban ruler whose reign began in 1946, photographed here in Nigeria, 1970.

Yoruban weaver.

long periods of intergroup warfare. One reason for this was the raiding of one Yoruba village by another to take people as slaves. Slavery existed among the Yoruba before trade with the Europeans. During the 1500s, Yoruba were taken as slaves to Brazil, in the 1600s they were taken to the Caribbean, and by the 1700s they were being shipped to North America.

When the Europeans began trading with the Yoruba in the

Yoruban woman having her hair plaited.

1800s, they introduced Christianity and European education. Throughout the century the Yoruba prospered but continued to war among themselves. Although Nigeria gained its independence from the British in 1960, the country continues to be plagued with conflicts between the Ibo and the Yoruba, and the Christians and the Muslims.

The Yoruba have always existed as a number of separate kingdoms, never being united under one great leader. Nevertheless, they had, and continue to have, great cultural unity. Today, the bulk of the Yoruba population—over 12 million people—resides in the

Carvings from a Yoruban door.

western part of Nigeria. In large cities such as Oyo, Lagos, and Iba-
dan, the Yoruba follow a Western lifestyle, working in air-condi-
tioned offices, shopping in supermarkets, and coping with the
tensions of crowded urban life. The rural Yoruba are spread out in
many small towns that dot the countryside. These towns, or *ilus,* are
enclosed by either a wall or a dirt embankment. Inside, interconnected compounds provide dwelling places for thousands of people.
The population in some towns is often greater than 15,000 people.
At the center is a royal palace and a marketplace. Each town has its

own government. Farm villages are called *aba* and are different from ilus in that they are temporary settlements rather than organized towns.

Traditional Yoruba homes are rectangular structures made of mud with triangular roofs of thatched palm leaves. The typical house has a sitting room as well as several bedrooms, a family room, and a kitchen with a fireplace. A yard and veranda with front posts carved in the form of horses and men complete the Yoruba dwelling. Furniture is usually simple—mats rather than beds or chairs. Today, many of the old compounds have been replaced by one- or two-story apartment buildings with corrugated metal roofs replacing the thatch. Along with agriculture, many Yoruba work as teachers, government officials, tailors, shopkeepers, builders, and business people in the larger cities.

Both women and men work, and women control their own earnings. A man may take more than one wife, but the women and their children inherit equally and a woman may get a divorce at any time. Inheritance rules have been affected by social conditions of the 20th century including a shortage of land. Today, property is divided among those sons who wish to work it, in contrast to past tradition in which property was shared by the entire family, with the oldest son assuming leadership of the extended families upon the patriarch's death.

Many Yoruba, especially those living in the larger cities, have adopted Western-style clothing. Traditional clothing included a sleeveless undervest, baggy pants, and a long cloth gown for the men. Women wore a wide piece of cloth hanging from the neck to the ankles, with a blouse extending to the waist; a thin veil and tie were worn around the head.

The Yoruba grow a variety of crops for the main staples of their diet: beans, yams, bananas, peanuts, cassava, plantain, maize, guinea corn, and palm oil (from which soup is made). Their most important crop is cocoa, which they export for cash. Yoruba specialties include fiery hot *eguisi* soup made from palm oil, vegetables, and peppers; grilled plantains; and deep-fried peanut balls.

The religious life of the Yoruba is varied. Most are Christian or Muslim, but some still practice their indigenous religious customs which include the belief in one supreme god and over 400 lesser gods, and the belief that ancestor spirits, called *orisa,* continue to influence the living. These followers use face masks, dances, music, rituals, and herbalists to soothe angry ancestor spirits.

The Yoruba are particularly well known for their artwork. They make use of many materials in their art, including wood, stone, terracotta, iron, copper, bronze, lead, brass, and ivory. Their ancient bronze castings found at Ife are counted among the masterpieces of the world. And they are famous for a complex method of casting metal known as the lost-wax method.

As is common with many other African cultures, much of Yoruba artwork is created for religious purposes. However, other items—jewelry and cooking vessels, for example—are made for decorative as well as practical reasons. Among the nonreligious artworks, wood carving has an important place. A common Yoruba statue is the *ibeji*, which celebrates the birth of twins. Ancient myths say that if one of the twins dies, the ibeji will take the place of the lost twin, so the two will always be a pair. In addition to art, the Yoruba in recent years have gained acclaim for their literature. One revered Yoruba writer, Wole Soyinka, won the Nobel Prize for literature in 1986.

In Togo the Yoruba are a minority ethnic group. In Benin and Nigeria they are one of the largest. In 1993, Ernest Shonekan, a Yoruba, became president of Nigeria.

ZULU
('zoo loo)

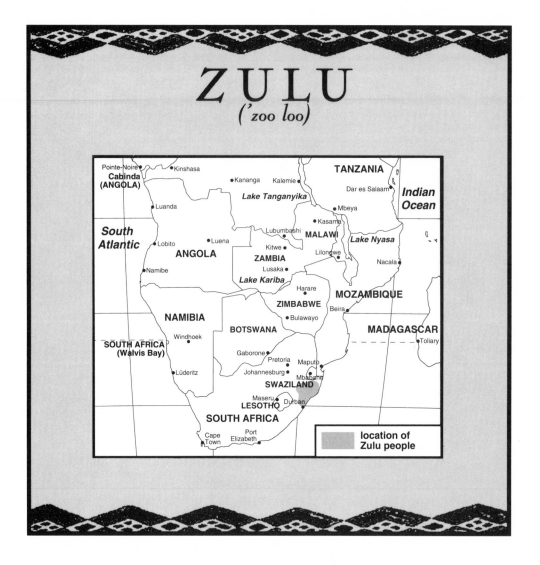

POPULATION:	2,500,000
LOCATION:	South Africa
LANGUAGES:	Zulu, Afrikaans, English
PRIMARY FOODS:	Cow milk and blood, millet, corn, pumpkin, yams, beans, meat

ONCE FEARED THROUGHOUT SOUTHERN AFRICA BECAUSE OF their brutal attacks on neighboring cultures, the Zulu reside in the Natal and Transvaal regions of South Africa. Most of the population lives in the 10,000-square-mile Zululand reserve along the Indian Ocean just north of the city of Durban. It is a semifertile area with a flat coastal plain, highlands to the west, and numerous rivers and streams. The subtropical climate brings lots of sunshine and brief but intense rain showers.

Descendants of the Nguni peoples of southeast Africa, the Zulu trace their history back to the 14th and 15th centuries when these peoples migrated southward and settled in modern-day South Africa. During the early 1800s, under the leadership of Zulu Chief Shaka, the Zulus established themselves as a powerful people. The Zulu army enlisted young men from all over the kingdom and trained them in warrior tactics using both throwing and stabbing spears. After crushing competing armies, and subjugating their people, Chief Shaka established a Zulu nation that was both feared and hated throughout southern Africa.

During the late 1800s, British troops invaded the Zulu territory and divided the land into 13 kingdoms, causing great dissent among the Zulu. In 1906 the Zulu attempted a rebellion against the British, but although they were accomplished warriors, they were no match for British gunfire. The Zulu never regained their independent power, and throughout the mid-1900s they were dominated by the white government of South Africa. In the late 1970s and early 1980s, the Zulu gained some rights to self-government but remained repressed by the minority white rule. Once self-sufficient, Zulu communities must now rely on employment outside the village in order to survive. Many men work in nearby towns or diamond mines to support their families.

A typical Zulu village is shaped like a horseshoe or circle, with a fence around the perimeter and a livestock pen in the center. Each village is made up of a very large extended family with a chief who serves as a leader. Most Zulu homes are shaped like a dome or beehive and are constructed of straw and grass. The floors are made of cow dung plaster. Some of the more modern homes are constructed of cement block with corrugated tin roofs.

Within traditional Zulu households, the father is given utmost

Mshiyeni Zulu, a Zulu paramount chief from the mid-1900s.

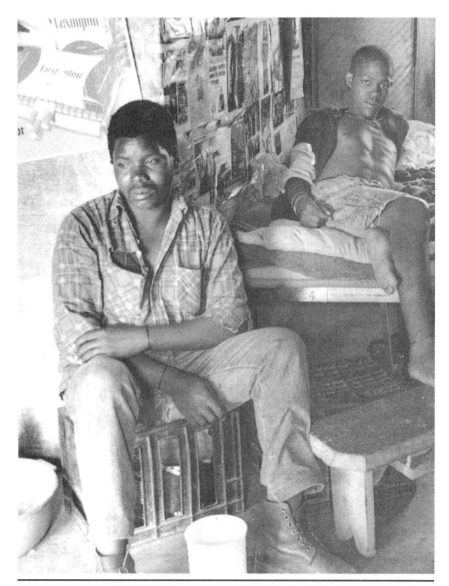

Young Zulu men in their house in South Africa.

respect. Children often fear their father and will not speak to him unless he speaks to them first. The mother's role is less authoritarian and more nurturing. It is the mother who passes Zulu folklore, history, and rules of behavior on to the children. If he can afford it, a Zulu man will take more than one wife.

Pattern from a Zulu woven mat from South Africa.

The division of labor between men and women is not an equal arrangement; women do a greater share of the work. This inequality stems from the days when Zulu men spent most of their time as warriors, and women were responsible for most chores in the home. Along with preparing food, cleaning, and caring for the children, women make repairs on the homes, collect water, carry and chop wood, make pots, weave baskets, and brew beer. Men clear the land of trees, construct the homes, and care for the livestock.

The Zulu diet consists mainly of cow products—such as milk, blood, and meat—millet, corn, yams, beans, and pumpkins. A pumpkin stew, with cinnamon and bits of meat, is a favorite meal. They also eat wild honey, yogurt, and melons and drink a chalky beer made from grain. Since large-scale farming on the reserves was disallowed for many years by the government, the Zulu in recent years have had to rely on processed foods that they get from trading with neighbors.

Zulu who work in urban areas wear Western-style clothing, but those who remain on the reserves continue to wear traditional dress. Traditional dress for the women is a long dress with a shawl. Married women wear black leather skirts and put a red clay tint in their hair, whereas young unmarried women wear their hair in a topknot. Traditional dress for men is a skirt made of animal skins and fur. During special ceremonies such as the Feast of First Fruits, a celebration of the new harvest, the men wear frilly white goatskin bands on their

Zulu carved wooden figure from South Africa.

arms and legs. Children, before they reach puberty, usually have their earlobes pierced with a piece of cornstalk. (Pierced ears represent a sign of maturity and the ability to listen and understand.) While courting, young men and women decorate themselves with feathers, animal skins, love charms, and colorful beads. These beads serve as love tokens, and each color represents a different message: white, love; green, resentment; black, unhappiness; and red, eyes weary from searching for a lost love.

Under the influence of British missionaries, many Zulu converted to Christianity, but many still practice their native religion. In Zulu religious life, great emphasis is placed on ancestor spirits. Offerings and sacrifices are made to these spirits for protection, health, and happiness. Because of this respect for ancestors, the Zulu believe that grave sites are sacred and must never be disturbed—angry spirits might cause harm. They also believe that ancestor spirits sometimes come back to the world in the form of snakes. If a snake appears in a Zulu village, the villagers make an animal sacrifice of a goat or lamb as an offering to show respect for the visiting snake spirit. The Zulu also believe in one supreme god, whom they call Unkulunkulu, but this god is thought to have less influence on their lives than the ancestor spirits.

Common Zulu design for hide shields.

Along with ancestor spirits, the Zulu believe in the use of magic. A bout of bad luck such as a poor harvest or a sore throat is considered to be the work of an angry spirit or someone placing a spell on them. When this happens, the Zulu solicit the help of an herbalist who uses natural remedies and prayers to get rid of the problem. Good magic, in the form of lucky charms and amulets, is often practiced by women. Members of a family are forbidden from practicing magic on each other.

Music, dance, and rituals play an important role in Zulu life. Birth, death, and marriage are all occasions for major celebrations that often include the ritual slaughter of an animal. Small goats are often raised expressly for this purpose. The beginning of a new harvest is also marked by major festivities. Dances are performed for many occasions and represent unity among the village. One special dance, performed by young men who are being initiated into manhood, is accompanied by thunderous drums; the men dress as warriors, wave their clubs, and thrust their cowhide shields forward in order to prove themselves to the chief. Songs are sung to praise members of the Zulu nation and to pass on oral histories. In addition to drums, the Zulu play stringed instruments made out of hollow gourds.

In recent years, the Zulu's struggle for better representation has led to many violent conflicts between the government police and other ethnic groups in South Africa. But the 1994 election of President Nelson Mandela means that the segregation and racial inequality they have endured will likely become a thing of the past.

Africa's Lost Cultures

THROUGHOUT THE LONG HISTORY OF AFRICA, MANY ANCIENT CIVILI-
zations thrived, rose to greatness and glory, and then slipped into
obscurity leaving few traces behind. Some of these cultures were
conquered by neighboring peoples; others just fell to ruin owing to
natural circumstances. In many parts of Africa, the harsh terrain and
scarcity of natural resources created fierce competition between
groups. There was only enough wealth from the land to support a
gradual increase in population. Thus, only some of the cultures were
able to rise to prominence, and almost always at the expense of
others.

With very little historical data to rely on, historians and anthropologists are still discovering facts and piecing together the stories
of Africa's ancient civilizations. Following are descriptions of five of
Africa's most fabled lost cultures. The maps on the left show the
areas they inhabited.

KUSH (kush)

The ancient kingdom of Kush centered on a city called Napata in
what is now Sudan. Although not much is known about the population or culture of the Kush, historians believe they were a wealthy
and powerful people as far back as the ninth century B.C. The Kushite civilization thrived for almost 1,000 years, leaving extensive but
largely unexcavated ruins of its monuments and villages.

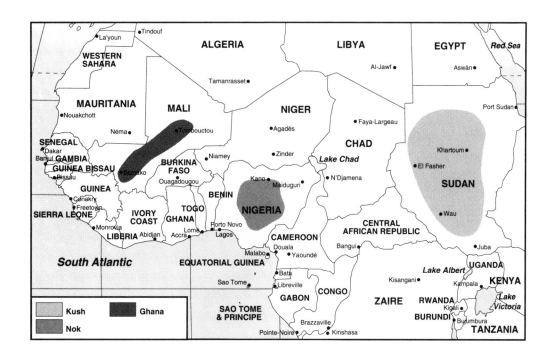

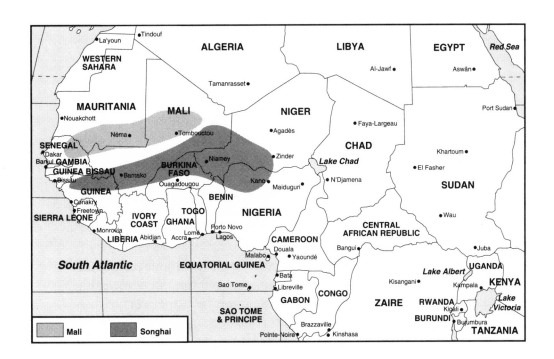

The Kush people were farmers and herders who traded with the ancient Egyptians. By the eighth century B.C., Kushite armies conquered most of Egypt, and for almost 100 years they dominated much of the African continent. But during the seventh century B.C., the powerful Assyrians invaded their territory, forcing the Kush to retreat up the Nile River and resettle in the ancient city of Meroë. From 500 B.C. to A.D. 200 the Kushites controlled a wide empire that was known throughout Africa for its iron tools and weapons.

But after A.D. 200, the Kush peoples began to lose their influence and strength, and by the year 700 the ancient Kush culture had faded from the continent. Historians believe that the Kush had a great influence on the developments of civilization in other parts of Africa. Some Ashanti and Yoruba legends refer to Kush ancestors who migrated from Kush territory to create new empires in West Africa.

NOK (knock)

The oldest culture of West Africa, the Nok peoples date back over 2,000 years. The Nok lived in the central regions of present-day Nigeria. What little information is available about the Nok comes from recovered artifacts such as stone and iron axes, remnants of ancient buildings, iron jewelry, tin beads, statues, and murals painted on cave walls.

Historians estimate that the Nok lived in Nigeria between 500 B.C. and A.D. 200. They were an agricultural society with organized villages of houses made of branches and dried mud. The language and population of the Nok are unknown. The land of the Nok was rich in gold, and along with cultivating crops, many Nok men worked as miners.

Evidence indicates that the Nok had a strong interest in art. Archaeologists have unearthed lifelike terra-cotta Nok statues that resemble the artwork of present-day Nigeria. These statues have elongated ears and heads that are three times larger than the bodies, a distortion which historians believe symbolized the Nok belief that the eyes and the ears were the most important parts of the human being.

Around 100 B.C., hunting and herding societies began to take control of most of the Nok region. These new societies established their own agricultural communities, and many of the Nok slowly merged with them. By about A.D. 200, the Nok became assimilated into these other societies, and their own social and economic unity dwindled. Eventually the Nok culture withered away.

GHANA ('gah nah)

The first great African empire south of the Sahara, the kingdom of Ghana was located along the Niger River in present-day Mali, about 700 miles north of the country of Ghana. It was the grandeur of ancient Ghana that inspired modern-day West Africans to name their country Ghana.

The kingdom of Ghana first rose to power around the sixth century. The population of the empire is unknown. Their language was Soninke, and their religion was based on ancestor and animal worship. Toward the later part of their history, many of the people

A bronze bracelet thought to be from the Ghana
Empire, Mali.

adopted Muslim traditions. The majority of the Ghanians were farmers, gold miners, and ironsmiths. During the medieval period, Ghana attracted students from Europe and Asia who came to study philosophy, medicine, and law at the many universities that flourished in the kingdom.

Most of the current information about the Ghanians comes from the writings of Arabs who traveled through their area. An eleventh-century Arab scholar wrote about the 200,000 Ghanian warriors he witnessed in the kingdom. These warriors, equipped with swords, daggers, and arrows, easily defeated enemies and overpowered neighboring kingdoms.

During their heyday, Ghanians carried on commerce with other parts of the world, trading gold, animal skins, ivory, kola nuts, honey, salt, cloth, copper and iron products. The kingdom was in the middle of a trading crossroad, and the Ghanians controlled this route by levying taxes on the traders.

The kingdom consisted of large, stone cities with central marketplaces that sold sacks of fruits, olives, dates, and grains. In addition to these foods, the Ghanians ate black-eyed peas and goat meat. In the northern part of the region the Ghanians lived in round earthen or thatched houses. In the south, Ghanian houses were built of thick slabs of salt with camel skin roofs.

Throughout their history, the Ghanians were threatened by many invaders. Finally, in 1203, they were attacked by King Sugmaguru Kante of Sosso, who seized the capital city of Ghana and forced many of the Ghanians into slavery for his own use and then sold many more. The capital city of Ghana was destroyed in 1240 by the king of Mali, and soon after the Ghana culture disappeared.

MALI ('mah lee)

While there are few written records that detail the ancient culture of Mali, it is believed that the empire was established by the leader Sundiata in the early 1200s. During its prosperous days the empire encompassed the areas of modern-day Mali, Mauritania, and Senegal. Mali contained the former empire of Ghana and was larger than all of Europe. As with Ghana, Mali's power came from gold, iron, and salt.

Mali included the famed ancient city of Timbuktu, which was the cultural center of the people. With a population of about 50,000, Timbuktu during the Mali empire was a bustling center of commerce with stone buildings and many libraries, schools, and shops. The Mali people spoke Mande and Arabic, and they practiced both indigenous African and the Muslim religions. The Mali economy was based on farming, herding, and mining for salt, gold, and copper. They traded these products with peoples from the East.

In 1307 Sundiata's grandson, Mansa Musa, became the sultan of Mali, and during his reign Mali became well-known throughout the Middle East and Europe as a rich and splendid empire. Following Mansa Musa's death, his son and then his brother ruled the kingdom for about another 50 years. Neither of them had the commanding leadership skills of Mansa Musa and therefore could not maintain the might of the kingdom. Mali began to decline, and eventually it divided into several smaller kingdoms, all of which fell prey to invading peoples. By the late 1400s, Timbuktu was taken over by the Songhai people, and by the mid-1600s the remaining Mali territories were conquered by Bambara armies. In the following century, what remained of the Mali culture was absorbed by the Mandinka kingdoms.

SONGHAI (song hi)

At its peak, the empire of Songhai stretched from the coast of the Atlantic Ocean in what is now Guinea eastward into parts of modern Niger and Nigeria. The ancient cities of Gao and Timbuktu served as the empire's main centers for commerce and culture.

After gaining control of the Mali empire during the 1400s, the Songhai peoples began to conquer neighboring groups and build their own empire. During the late 1400s, the Songhai empire prospered under the leadership of Sunni Ali, a ruthless and powerful man who was known to be an expert at sorcery. Although his Songhai government was brutally repressive, Sunni Ali established a powerful empire that would last for over 100 years.

In the empire's early years, most of the Songhai were farmers, fishermen, and shipbuilders. As the empire progressed, more and more of the people became merchants who traded in the empire's bustling market districts. They also grew wealthy from the region's gold and salt mines.

The Songhai peoples were Muslims, but many also followed ancient African religious customs. They spoke both Songhai and Arabic. In the large city of Gao, the Songhai lived in stone buildings; in the rural areas they lived in dome-shaped thatch houses. The population of the Songhai is unknown.

In 1591, Moroccan troops, equipped with guns and cannons, marched into Songhai, captured Gao and Timbuktu, and claimed the gold and salt mines for themselves. Having only spears and arrows to fight back with, the Songhai were easily overpowered. Eventually the Songhai empire crumbled and was taken over by more powerful empires such as the Hausa, Fulani, and Bambara.

APPENDIX

Additional African Cultures

CULTURE	LOCATION
Acholi	Uganda
Adja	Benin
Aduma	Gabon
Agni	Ivory Coast
Ahanta	Ghana
Aizo	Benin
Akan	Ghana
Akposo	Togo
Alar	Zaire
Ambo	Southern Africa
Ana	Togo
Anaak	Sudan, Ethiopia
Bagisu	Uganda
Bakele	Gabon
Bakiga	Uganda
Bakota	Gabon
Balante	Guinea-Bissau
Bambara	Mali
Bamileke	Cameroon
Banda	Central African Republic
Banyaruanda	Uganda
Banziri	Central African Republic
Baoulé	Ivory Coast

CULTURE	LOCATION
Barwe	Zimbabwe
Basoga	Uganda
Bateke	Congo
Batoro	Uganda
Beja	Sudan, Ethiopia
Beri	Sudan
Beriberi-Manga	Niger
Bete	Ivory Coast
Beti	Cameroon
Bini	Nigeria
Bobo	Burkina Faso
Bokora	Uganda
Bomvana	South Africa
Bopgandi	Zaire
Bor	Sudan
Bunga	Central African Republic
Bunji	Zimbabwe
Bwaka	Zaire
Chaga	Tanzania
Chamba	Togo
Chewas	Malawi
Dagomba	Ghana
Daju	Chad
Damara	Namibia
Dan	Ivory Coast
Danakil	Ethiopia
Dialonke	Guinea
Diola	Senegal
Djerma	Niger
Dodoth	Uganda
Duma	Zimbabwe
Dumara	Namibia
Edo	Nigeria
Enenga	Gabon
Evalue	Ghana
Fanti	Ghana

CULTURE	LOCATION
Fingo	South Africa
Fula	Gambia
Fungwe	Zimbabwe
Ga	Ghana
Galla	Ethiopia, Kenya
Galoa	Gabon
Gogo	Tanzania
Golla	Liberia
Gonja	Ghana
Govera	Zimbabwe
Gurma	Togo
Guro	Ivory Coast
Gurunsi	Burkina Faso
Gusii	Kenya
Gwena	Zimbabwe
Ha	Tanzania
Haya	Tanzania
Hehe	Tanzania
Hlubi	South Africa
Hutu	Burundi, Rwanda
Ibibio	Nigeria
Igala	Nigeria
Igbo	Nigeria
Ijan	Nigeria
Ila	Zambia
Isaa	Djibouti
Iteso	Uganda
Jie	Uganda
Jola	Gambia
Jonaam	Zaire, Uganda
Kabrai	Togo
Kalenjin	Kenya
Kanuari	Niger
Kaoko	Namibia
Karamojong	Uganda
Karanga	Zimbabwe

Culture	Location
Kavango	Namibia
Keiyo	Kenya
Kimbundo	Angola
Kipsigis	Kenya
Kirdi	Chad
Kissi	West Africa
Koranki	Guinea
Korekore	Zimbabwe
Kotokoli	Togo
Kpele	Guinea, Liberia
Krim	West Africa
Kunari	Nigeria
Kwakwa	Ivory Coast
Lamba	Togo
Lango	Uganda
Lebu	Senegal
Lega	Central Africa
Leya	Zimbabwe
Lilima	Zimbabwe
Limba	West Africa
Lobi	Burkina Faso
Loko	West Africa
Loso	Togo
Lozi	Zambia
Luba	Zaire
Luhya	Kenya
Lunda	Zaire
Lungu	South Africa
Luo	Kenya, Tanzania
Luvale	Zambia
Maba	Chad
Makonde	Tanzania
Makua	Mozambique
Mandjia	Central African Republic
Mandyako	Guinea-Bissau
Marakwet	Kenya

CULTURE	LOCATION
Marka	Mali, Niger
Marya	Ethiopia
Matheniko	Uganda
Matopo	Zimbabwe
Mbaka	Central African Republic
Mboshi	Congo
Mbum	Central African Republic
Mbunda	Angola
Mende	Sierra Leone
Mensa	Ethiopia
Mesarit	Chad
Mholo	South Africa
Mina	Togo
Minianka	Mali, Niger
Moba	Togo
Mongo	Zaire
Moshi	Ghana
Mossi	Burkina Faso
Mpondo	South Africa
Mwera	Tanzania
Nama	Namibia
Nanzwa	Zimbabwe
Ndau	Zimbabwe
Ngonia	Zambia
Ngqika	South Africa
Nguni	South Africa
Nohwe	Zimbabwe
Nubia	Sudan
Nuer	Sudan
Nupe	Nigeria
Nyai	Zimbabwe
Nyakyusa	South Africa
Nyamwezi	Tanzania
Nyubi	Zimbabwe
Nzima	Ghana
Okande	Gabon

CULTURE	LOCATION
Oromo	Ethiopia, Kenya
Orungu	Gabon
Ovambo	Angola, Namibia
Ovimbundu	Angola
Padhola	Uganda
Pakot	Kenya
Parpels	Guinea-Bissau
Peul	Mali
Pian	Uganda
Pokot	Kenya
Pondo	Southern Africa
Sabaot	Kenya
Salamat	Chad
Sanga	Congo
Sara	Chad, Central African Republic
Sarakole	Mauritania
Seke	Gabon
Senufo	Ivory Coast, Mali, Niger
Serahuli	Gambia
Serer	Senegal
Shabi	Zimbabwe
Shambaa	Tanzania
Shangaan	Mozambique
Shankili	Ethiopia
Sherbo	West Africa
Shilluk	Sudan
Shira	Gabon
Shona	Zimbabwe, Mozambique
Somali	Ethiopia, Kenya
Somba	Benin
Songe	Zaire
Soso	West Africa
Sotho	Lesotho (South Africa)
Sukama	Tanzania
Susu	Guinea
Swazi	Swaziland (South Africa)

CULTURE	LOCATION
Tatog	Tanzania
Tawara	Zimbabwe
Teda	Chad
Tembu	Southern Africa
Teme	Sierra Leone
Terik	Kenya
Themba	South Africa
Tigrai	Ethiopia
Tiv	Nigeria, Cameroon
Toma	Guinea
Tubu	Niger
Tugen	Kenya
Tuken	Kenya
Tukulor	Senegal, Mauritania
Turkana	Kenya
Twa	Burundi, Rwanda
Twi	Ghana
Ungwe	Zimbabwe
Vai	Liberia, Sierra Leone
Venda	South Africa
Wati	Togo
Xhosa	South Africa
Yao	Malawi, Tanzania, Mozambique
Zalamo	Tanzania
Zande	Central African Republic, Zaire
Zezuru	Zimbabwe
Zigula	Tanzania

Glossary

AGE-SET: A social grouping within a culture based on age.

AMULET: A good luck charm.

ANIMISM: The belief that spirits live in natural objects such as trees, rivers, and stones. Animists perform ceremonies to please these spirits so that the spirits will protect them from harm.

APARTHEID: An official policy of separation of South Africans into racial categories of white, black, Asian, and colored people of mixed races.

BEDOUIN: A nomadic Arab.

BERBERS: Descendants of ancient peoples from northwestern Africa near the Mediterranean coast.

BRIDE-PRICE: Money paid to the bride or her family, usually by the husband's family, before marriage.

CASH CROP: Agriculture raised for income.

CAUCASIAN/CAUCASOID: Relating to the white race of humankind as classified according to physical features.

CIRCUMCISION: Ceremonial removal of a part of male or female genital organs as a rite of adulthood.

CLAN: A subgroup of people within a tribe.

DUNG: Dried animal excrement.

EXTENDED FAMILY: A family group that is made up of parents, children, aunts, uncles, cousins, and grandparents.

INDIGENOUS: Having originated and living naturally in a particular region or environment.

INFANTICIDE: The killing of newborn babies and infants who are sick or weak.

KIN: A group of people of common ancestry.

KORAN: The Muslim book of religious revelations.

KRAAL: A pen for holding livestock; also used to describe a small village of native Africans.

MAIZE: Corn.

MANIOC: The starchy root of the cassava plant used in food.

MATRIARCHY: A system of social organization in which descent and inheritance are traced through the female line.

MATRILINEAL: A family structure that traces descent through the mother's heritage.

MILLET: A grass cultivated for its grain which is used for food.

MONOTHEISM: The belief and worship of one god.

MOSQUE: A building used for public worship by Muslims.

NOMADS: People who move from place to place and have no permanent home.

PANTHEISM: The belief and worship of many gods.

PAPYRUS: A water plant that grows mainly in the Nile River region and is used to create paperlike material.

PASTORAL: Devoted to the raising of livestock.

PATRIARCHY: A system of social organization marked by the supremacy of the father in the family, in which descent and inheritance are traced through the male line.

PATRILINEAL: A family structure that traces descent through the father's heritage.

PIDGIN: A simplified speech used for communication between people with different languages.

PLANTAIN: A tropical fruit plant similar to the banana.

POLYGYNY: The practice of having more than one wife at one time.

PYGMIES: Short, dwarflike people of equatorial Africa.

SAVANNA: A flat, treeless grassland.

SCARIFICATION: The cutting or scratching of the skin to produce scars.

SEMITES: People of Arab or Jewish heritage.

SISAL: A tough, white fiber used to make rope.

SORGHUM: A tall canelike plant that provides sweet juice.

STEPPE: A large, slightly wooded, semiarid grassy plain.

SUBTRIBE: A tribe within a tribe.

TEFF: A grain cereal.

TERRA-COTTA: A reddish brown clay used for statues and pottery.

TORAH: The Jewish book of religious laws and traditions.

TUBER: A fleshy plant root.

VELD: A grassland with scattered shrubs and trees.

WATTLE: Building material composed of poles, branches, reeds and twigs.

WESTERN-STYLE: Customs practiced in Europe and the Western Hemisphere.

Selected Bibliography

Addison, John. *Ancient Africa.* New York: John Day, 1970.

Africa South of the Sahara. 20th edition. London: Europa Publications, 1990.

Allen, William D., and Jerry E. Jennings. *Africa.* Grand Rapids, Mich.: Fideler, 1986.

Amin, Mohamed, ed. *Insight Guide: Kenya.* Singapore: Apa Publications, 1992.

Argyle, W. J. *The Fon of Dahomey.* Oxford: Clarendon Press, 1966.

Asher, Michael. *A Desert Dies.* New York: St. Martin's Press, 1986.

Bethwell, Georges, and Jacques Maquet. *Dictionary of Black African Civilization.* New York: Leon Amiel, 1974.

Boahen, Adu. *Topics in West African History.* London: Longman, 1966.

Buchholzr, John. *The Land of the Burnt Faces.* New York: Robert M. McBride, 1956.

Caputo, Robert. "Ethiopia: Revolution in an Ancient Empire." *National Geographic,* May 1983, pp. 614–45.

Crowther, Geoff. *Africa on a Shoestring.* Australia: Lonely Planet, 1989.

Davidson, Basil. *Africa in History.* New York: Macmillan, 1974.

———. *The Black Man's Burden: Africa and the Case of the Nation State.* New York: Random House, 1992.

———. *The Lost Cities of Africa.* Boston: Little, Brown, 1987.

Eades, J. S. *The Yoruba Today.* Cambridge: Cambridge University Press, 1980.

Englebert, Victor. "Drought Threatens the Tuareg World." *National Geographic.* April 1974, pp. 544–71.

Frederikse, Julie. *South Africa: A Different Kind of War.* Boston: Beacon Press, 1986.

Gailey, Harry A. *History of Africa from 1800 to the Present.* New York: Holt, Rinehart and Winston, 1972.

Gamble, David P. *Ethnographic Survey of Africa: The Wolof of Sengambia.* London: International African Institute, 1967.

Gruber, Ruth. *Rescue: The Exodus of the Ethiopian Jews.* New York: Macmillan, 1987.

Haape, Johannes, ed. *Insight Guide: Namibia.* Singapore: Apa Publications, 1993.

Hilton, Anne. *The Kingdom of Kongo.* Oxford: Oxford University Press, 1985.

Hultman, Tami, ed. *Africa News Cookbook.* New York: Penguin, 1986.

Imperato, Pascal James. *Historical Dictionary of Mali.* Metuchen, N.J.: Scarecrow, 1977.

July, Robert W. *A History of the African People.* New York: Charles Scribner's Sons, 1974.

Lane, Martha S. B. *Malawi.* Chicago: Children's Press, 1990.

Laure, Jason. *Zimbabwe.* Chicago: Children's Press, 1988.

Lystad, Robert A. *The Ashanti: A Proud People.* Greenwich, Conn.: Greenwood Press, 1968.

MacGaffey, Wyatt. *Art and Healing of the Bakongo.* Stockholm: Folksen Museum Etnografiska, 1991.

Martin, Phyllis M. *Historical Dictionary of Angola.* Metuchen, N.J.: Scarecrow, 1980.

Morris, Donald R. *Washing the Spears: The Rise and Fall of the Zulu Nation.* New York: Simon and Schuster, 1986.

Morton, Fred, et al. *Historical Dictionary of Botswana.* Metuchen, N.J.: Scarecrow, 1989.

Moss, Joyce, and George Wilson. *Peoples of the World: Africans South of the Sahara.* Detroit: Gale Research, 1991.

Oliver, Ronald, and Michael Crowder, ed. *The Cambridge Encyclopedia of Africa.* Cambridge: Cambridge University Press, 1981.

Pohlmann, Wolfger, ed. *amaNdebele.* Tübingen, Germany: Ernst Wasmuth Tübinger, 1991.

Rapaport, Louis. *Lost Jews: Last of the Ethiopian Falashas.* New York: Stein and Day, 1980.

Roscoe, The Reverend John. *The Baganda.* London: Frank Cass, 1965.

Schapera, I. *The Tswana.* Plymouth, England: Clark, Doble and Brendon, 1976.

Smail, J. L. *From the Land of the Zulu Kings.* Durban, South Africa: A. J. Pope, 1979.

Smith, Robert. *Kingdoms of the Yoruba.* London: Methuen, 1969.

Sudan, A Country Study. Area handbook series. Washington, D.C.: American University, 1982.

Volmer, Jurgen. *Black Genesis: African Roots.* New York: St. Martin's Press, 1980.

Index

Note: Main entries for individual tribes do not appear in the index, as tribes are arranged in alphabetical order in the text.